A KING'S COLONEL AT NIAGARA, 1774-1776

LT. COL. JOHN CALDWELL AND THE BEGINNINGS OF THE AMERICAN REVOLUTION ON THE NEW YORK FRONTIER

by

PAUL L. STEVENS

OLD FORT NIAGARA

OLD FORT NIAGARA ASSOCIATION, Inc.
YOUNGSTOWN, NEW YORK
©1987

ISBN Number: 0-941967-05-0

This publication has been funded, in part, by a donation from Ferguson Electric Construction Co., Inc., Buffalo, New York.

For Cindy and Charlie

TABLE OF CONTENTS

Regimental color of the 8th (King's) Regiment of Foot. *Drawing by Marbud Prozeller.*

Lt. Col. Caldwell's America
1774 - 1776

Map by Marbud Prozeller.

4

The King's Regiment Comes to Niagara

Throughout the War for American Independence, New York's rebels had to contend with British opponents deployed at the three corners of their infant state. Along New York's northern border, royal troops kept their grip on Laurentian Canada (the former French settlements bordering the St. Lawrence River) throughout the conflict despite one nearly successful effort to dislodge them. To the southward, the king's commanders captured New York City and its environs in September, 1776, and remained there until November, 1783, with a large force of British, German, and loyalist regiments and Royal navy warships. With only a handful of companies and small schooners, crown officials far to the west also held the Niagara Frontier from 1775 through 1783 and beyond. During those years Fort Niagara is most often noted for its role as the home base for the Indian and loyalist raiders who ravaged the New York and Pennsylvania frontiers from late 1777 through mid-1782,[1] and its few prominent Revolutionary-era figures are those who led these raiders. Books and articles—non-fiction and fiction, accurate and wildly inaccurate— have appeared to relate the exploits of loyalist officer John Butler, his son Walter, and their corps of rangers,[2] to recite the adventures of the Mohawk war chief Thayendanegea (Joseph Brant),[3] and to recount the diplomacy of Indian superintendent Guy Johnson.[4]

Of the men who actually commanded the royal establishment at Niagara, conversely, little has been written. Only Lieutenant Colonel Mason Bolton, who presided there from 1777 to 1780 and died in a tragic

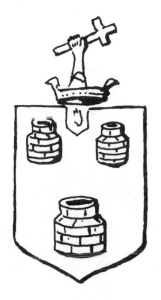

The Caldwell coat of arms. The motto was *Sapere aude (Dare to Know)*. *Drawing by Marbud Prozeller.*

shipwreck on Lake Ontario, has been subjected to any historical inquiry. He left sufficient correspondence in the papers of Quebec governor, Lieutenant General Frederick Haldimand, for Frank H. Severance to prepare an account of his tenure at Niagara more than eighty years ago.[5]

Several of Niagara's other Revolutionary-era commandants are known to history largely through their activities elsewhere. For example, Brigadier General Henry Watson Powell, senior officer at Niagara during 1780-1782, is more often recognized for his service in 1777 as commander of one of Burgoyne's brigades and as defender of Ticonderoga against counterattacking American militia.[6] Brigadier General Allan Maclean, Niagara's officer-in-charge during 1782-1783, is sometimes remembered for his ticklish war-closing diplomacy with both the Iroquois and the Americans, but his renown rests on his creation of the Royal Highland Emigrants Regiment in 1775 and his staunch defense of Quebec City against rebel invaders.[7] Lieutenant Colonel Arent S. De Peyster com-manded Niagara from June, 1784, through June, 1785, but only his activities as military commandant of Michilimackinac (1774-1779) and Detroit (1779-1784) and his friendship in retirement with Scottish poet Robert Burns have received any scholarly attention.[8] Regarding two commandants, Lieutenant Colonel Robert Hoyes (1783-1784) and Lieutenant Colonel John Caldwell, furthermore, practically nothing is known. This situation is particularly regretable in respect to Caldwell because this officer governed western New York and, in fact, exercised military authority over most of the northwestern frontier during the crucial, turbulent years when colonial protest burst into armed rebellion.

John Caldwell's service at Niagara occurred, unfortnately, during a period when circumstances combined to limit greatly the amount of official paperwork to survive for later examination. Prior to the fighting in April, 1775, Caldwell reported directly to Britain's North American commander-in-chief headquartered at New York City and later at Boston. Distance, poor weather, and growing civil unrest, however, resulted in an uncertainty and hence infrequency of correspondence. No sooner had Caldwell been ordered to report instead to the governor of Quebec Province, furthermore, than Continental armies invaded the St. Lawrence Valley, first disrupting and then severing entirely his communications with that official. That governor, moreover, was Lieutenant General Guy Carleton, an aloof and intensely private man, who, unlike his successor Haldimand, ordered that his personal papers be destroyed at the time of his death.[9] With them were lost almost all of the few reports he had received from the western posts during the early years of the Revolution. Finally, the voluminous inter-post cor-

A lieutenant colonel, 8th (King's) Regiment of Foot, 1774-1776. *Drawing by Eric Manders.*

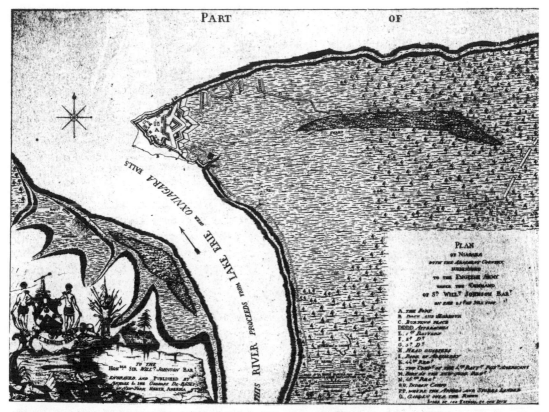

British forces took Fort Niagara from the French in 1759 after a siege of nineteen days. *Courtesy, The New-York Historical Society, New York.*

respondence, which is known to have passed among Britain's frontier forts and which centered at Niagara, has disappeared almost entirely. In consequence, Caldwell's pivotal role at Niagara has gone largely unreported in the extant written record.

Nevertheless, source materials do exist in sufficient quantity and variety to permit investigation of many aspects of Colonel Caldwell's administration of Niagara. In particular, they reveal the problems Caldwell faced and the policies he followed at a time when both were changing constantly on the British frontier. Additionally, they disclose the methods by which he attempted to support the royal interest in the contest between loyalists and rebels in New York's Mohawk Valley. They also show the

many responsibilities that devolved upon Caldwell not only as Niagara's commandant but as Britain's senior military official west of Montreal at a time when events cut off the west from royal orders and supplies. In meeting the many administrative, military, and diplomatic challenges thrust upon him by the colonial rebel-

Enlisted men of the King's Regiment wore distinctive pewter buttons on their coats. Examples of both types have been recovered at sites occupied by the unit from 1774 to 1785. *Drawings by Marbud Prozeller.*

lion, Caldwell typified the handful of regular officers who headed or would later head the garrisons scattered across the northern interior. Especially in his preparation for commanding an isolated American outpost in wartime, he reflected the inadequate background of most British officers. Yet he also matched these frontier commanders in his ability to adapt to unfamiliar circumstances and to learn from his experience.

Like many other officers in the king's service, John Caldwell was a younger son of British aristocracy. His father, Sir John Caldwell, was the third Irish Baronet Caldwell of Castle Caldwell in County Fermanagh. Sir John's six sons all sought careers in the military, the eldest, James, serving in the Austrian army before succeeding to the family's title and small estate in northern Ireland. Of the other five, four—John, Hume, Henry, and Frederick—became army officers, and a fifth, Charles, gained a commission in the Royal Navy.

John, the family's second son (born about 1725), spent the formative years of his career with the 7th Regiment of Foot (Royal Fusiliers), in which he eventually gained a captaincy in December, 1755. Soon afterward, the Fusiliers joined Admiral John Byng's fleet as marines and participated in his battle against the French off Minorca in May, 1756. They were then put ashore at Gibraltar, where they—and Caldwell—served with the garrison throughout the Seven Years' War. They did not return to England until 1763. From 1765 through early 1770 the 7th was headquartered at Fort George, Scotland, where Caldwell became the regiment's major in July, 1766. The Fusiliers' transfer to barracks at Chatham in Kent put Caldwell closer to the army's administrative center in London, and he began to seek another promotion. By summer 1772 he had hopes of purchasing the lieutenant colonelcy of his own regiment, but the vacancy did not occur. Instead, he bought the lieutenant colonelcy of the 8th (King's) Regiment of Foot, his new commission being dated October 27, 1772. Up to that point, Caldwell had seen duty, except for the war years at Gibraltar, only at homecountry garrisons in Ireland, Scotland, and England. His new regiment, however, was then stationed far across the Atlantic in Canada.[10]

The 8th (King's) Regiment had been in the Province of Quebec since 1768 performing garrison duty at Quebec City's citadel and at various

A soldier of the 8th Regiment of Foot loads his "Brown Bess" musket. *Drawing by David Abbott.*

small posts throughout the St. Lawrence Valley. Like all other British regiments, its colonel-in-chief, major General Bigoe Armstrong, left the regiment's actual field command to its lieutenant colonel. Caldwell, therefore, could waste little time in joining it, which he did during the summer or autumn of 1773. Aged about fifty, unmarried, and arriving in North America for the first time, he found himself not entirely among strangers. The Royal Fusiliers had been sent to join the British forces in Canada that spring, and Caldwell was able to dine at Quebec with his old messmates.

Caldwell probably also encountered his younger brother Henry briefly during his stay in the city. As a junior officer, Henry Caldwell had campaigned with General James Wolfe against the French at Louisbourg and Quebec during the French and Indian War. Reaching the rank of "major in America" in 1772, he returned home sometime during the following year and retired from the army. In 1774, however, he brought his newly-wed Irish wife back to Canada and settled upon large estates that included several leased *seigneuries,* farms, gristmills, and a house in the Quebec suburb of Ste. Foye. He also enjoyed the friendship of Quebec's Governor Carleton, whose wartime assistant he had been in the quartermaster department. Colonel Caldwell's reunion with family and friends lasted a few months at most, however, because early in 1774 he was ordered to lead the King's Regiment up the St. Lawrence into Indian territory.[11]

At that time Britain maintained only five isolated outposts in the vast hinterland west of Quebec Province and the Appalachians and north of the Ohio River. Four of them guarded strategic narrows along the two great water routes over which flowed the

Maj. Gen. Frederick Haldimand acted as commander-in-chief in North America during the absence of Lt. Gen. Thomas Gage in 1773-1774. Haldimand had served in the Niagara campaign of 1759 but performed his most notable service as Governor of Quebec from 1778 to 1784. *Courtesy, Public Archives of Canada, C-3221.*

lucrative fur trade of the north: the St. Lawrence River-lower Great Lakes waterway that connected the markets at Quebec, Montreal, and Albany with the Indian tribes of the midwest; and the Ottawa River highway that led from Montreal to the upper Great Lakes and the rich peltry grounds around the upper Mississippi. The smallest post, Oswegatchie (present Ogdensburg, N.Y.), stood on the south bank of the St. Lawrence near the La Gallette rapids, where merchandise was transferred between the bateaux that plied the river and the ships that sailed Lake Ontario. The largest post, Fort Niagara, guarded the crucial portage around Niagara Falls connecting Lakes Ontario and Erie. The crown also kept a military garrison at the substantial *Canadien* (Franco-American) settlement at Detroit, astride the river-

Capt. Arent Schuyler De Peyster. *Courtesy, the King's Regiment Collection, National Museums and Galleries on Merseyside.*

way joining Lakes Erie and Huron. A small palisaded fort at Michilimackinac, on the southern shore of the straits between Lakes Huron and Michigan, protected that entrepôt for the peltry trade of the far west. The fifth post was located near the confluence of the Ohio and Mississippi Rivers at the *Canadien* village of Kaskaskia, where two lonely companies of redcoats represented the only crown authority in the Illinois-Wabash country.[12]

The western garrisons were due for rotation in 1774. Soldiers of the 18th (Royal Irish) Regiment of Foot had held the Illinois country since 1768, but civil unrest in the east and Indian troubles in the upper Ohio Valley prevented sending a detachment to relieve Captain Hugh Lord and his men at Kaskaskia. On the other hand, the four more-accessible posts on the Great Lakes were all garrisoned by the 10th Regiment of Foot, which had manned them for the requisite two years. Consequently, in February,

1774, General Haldimand, then at New York City acting as commander-in-chief during the temporary absence of Lieutenant General Thomas Gage in England, selected the 8th Regiment to replace the 10th.

In many ways Caldwell's regiment was better qualified than most British units for such duty. Six years in Canada had acclimated its men to the country and to some of the mundane duties required at the upper posts, such as handling bateaux. In organization and numbers, however, it resembled all other regiments on Britain's peacetime establishment. It was made up of ten companies: eight center or battalion companies and two elite flank companies (one of grenadiers and one of light infantry). At peacetime strength it was authorized 477 men, each company having a captain, 2 lieutenants, 2 sergeants, 3 corporals, 38 privates, and 2 drummers (plus 2 fifers for the grenadiers), and the remainder comprising the field and staff officers. Yet regiments stationed in America rarely maintained their full complement of men, and Caldwell probably had 450 or fewer in the regiment he took west in 1774. The majority of his rank and file, however, seem to have been experienced soldiers in their twenties and thirties who had already served from five to fifteen years. His senior officers, moreover, were experienced in the army and in Canada and, of greater importance, were competent and versatile. One young officer, Durell Saumarez, considered himself lucky to have joined the King's because, he declared, "we have a set of very gentill officers."[13]

Sometime in March Caldwell received from Lieutenant Colonel Valentine Jones, then senior British officer in Quebec, Haldimand's instructions regarding the King's Regiment. Caldwell was ordered to embark his troops in two divisions, the first five companies to depart Montreal for the most distant outposts as soon as the St. Lawrence became free of ice and the five remaining companies to set out as soon afterward as additional transport could be arranged. Caldwell promptly selected the officers who would command the various garrisons, directed the detachments then stationed at Chambly and other Canadian posts to assemble at Montreal at once, and led the companies at Quebec upriver to a staging area at Trois Rivières.[14]

Led by Captains Richard B. Lernoult and Arent S. De Peyster, the first division embarked in bateaux at Lachine during the third week of May and arrived at Detroit at the beginning of July. Three battalion companies remained at Detroit under Lernoult, who merited the command of this most populous western settlement by his position as the 8th's third-ranking captain, the most senior officer available (the regiment's major and second captain being absent from America, and its senior captain, elderly James Webb, remaining with Caldwell as adjutant). The captain fourth in seniority, De Peyster, took command at Michilimackinac on July 10 with one battal-

Brass waistbelt buckle, 8th Regiment of Foot, 1774-1785, excavated at Old Fort Niagara.

ion company and the grenadier company.[15] Caldwell himself led the second division into Montreal on June 4 and into the bateaux at Lachine four days later. On June 17 these five companies reached Oswegatchie, where Caldwell detached the light infantry company under George Forster, the King's sixth-ranking captain. For six weeks, however, contrary winds prevented Caldwell from obtaining passage on a sailing vessel. He was not able to cross Lake Ontario with his four companies and reach his new headquarters at Fort Niagara until the first week in August.[16]

Although interrupted by the portage around its famous cataracts, the Niagara River provided the most direct route to the heart of the continent. Viewed from the air, the broad lower river suddenly constricts at the mouth of the Niagara gorge. Fort Niagara is visible at the mouth of the river and the mist rising from the Falls at the upper right. *Courtesy, New York Power Authority.*

The "Most Desert Part" of the Continent

On August 7, 1774, Lieutenant Colonel John Caldwell assumed command of Fort Niagara from Lieutenant Colonel Francis Smith, who took his 10th Regiment back to Quebec and later to Massachusetts, where he would next command a British column marching against villages named Lexington and Concord.[17] Meanwhile, Caldwell surveyed the place he had to defend with the fewer than 200 regulars of his four companies of the King's Regiment. Niagara, the strongest British fortification in the west,[18] stood on a point of land on the eastern shore at the Niagara River's juncture with Lake Ontario. The French had built it to control the Niagara portage route through which funneled most travel to the four western lakes, but the British had seized it after a bloody siege in 1759.[19]

Extensive earthworks and palisades protected the landward base of Niagara's triangular battlements, but only a row of pickets guarded the sides overlooking the river and the lake. Five bastions, two new stone redoubts, a large stone edifice (known today as the "French Castle"), and an interior stockade provided strongpoints, but the fort had deteriorated under the control of a parsimonious British government. Decaying pickets and slumping ramparts had left its outer walls almost defenseless, especially since the entire sprawling works required a garrison of perhaps one thousand to be properly manned. Even the commandant's own house, a wooden structure located in the outer fort near the lakeside palisade, had a rotting, leaky roof.[20]

Unlike Detroit, Michilimackinac and Kaskaskia, which had substantial civilian populations, Fort Niagara was entirely a military post. Only a few Indian traders kept houses and stores on "the Bottoms," as the flats between the fort and the riverbank were known. Across the river from the fort, however, a building called Navy Hall served as a center for constructing, repairing and wintering the few armed vessels that sailed Lake Ontario under the direction of the military's naval department. In 1774 the crown's Lake Ontario fleet comprised merely the 18-gun snow *Haldimand* and the sloop *Charity,* which carried only six small swivel guns. In addition, materials were then being gathered to construct two smaller sailing craft at the yards at Navy Hall and Oswegatchie. Two other royal vessels, the 16-gun schooner *Gage* and the 12-gun schooner *Dunmore,* and a half-dozen private schooners and sloops, owned by merchants at Detroit and Michilimackinac, sailed Lakes Erie and Huron and connected Niagara with the westernmost posts. Although Britain's North American commander-in-chief controlled the naval department and Alexander Grant, styled "Commodore" Grant, supervised the king's shipping from Detroit, Niagara's commandant had authority to direct the vessels' movements whenever necessary.[21]

In 1764 the Iroquois Indians had granted to the British the use of a four-mile strip of land along each side of the Niagara River's entire length. In this area Fort Niagara had three dependent posts, which acted as transfer points along the portage and which each demanded protection by some of Caldwell's redcoats. At the river's lower landing beneath the Niagara escarpment, British engineers had constructed a tramway-lift sys-

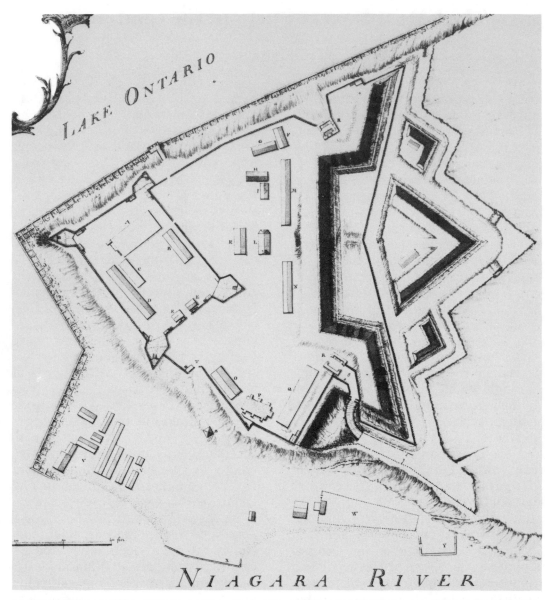

Lt. Francis Pfister's "Plan of Niagara with an Explanation of its present State" was completed on September 28, 1773. It best represents Fort Niagara at the time of Caldwell's arrival. His quarters were in the building labeled "F" at top center. *Courtesy, British Library, Crown Maps, cxxi, 76.*

tem (known as the "Cradles") in 1764 to carry cargoes between the eastern shore and the northern terminus of the portage on the cliff above. Caldwell periodically had to send a corporal's guard to watch over the log storehouses there when a ship tied up to on-load or off-load. At the southern terminus of the portage road stood the small picketted work of Fort Schlosser (or Little Niagara). This was headquarters for John, Philip, and Charles Stedman, brothers to whom the crown had granted a monopoly to operate the portage road and its carriage, subject to the orders of Niagara's commandant. Because the Stedmans and their employees maintained the place, Caldwell had only to station a sergeant and squad

Ens. Henry De Berniere of the 10th Regiment sketched Fort Niagara in 1773. The vessel moored at Navy Hall is almost certainly the snow *Haldimand*. *Courtesy, National Army Museum, London.*

of regulars there to watch over the bateaux that carried cargoes along the upper river between Schlosser and Fort Erie. Fort Erie, a small palisaded post located on the western shore at the entrance to Lake Erie, was little more than a warehouse for storing merchandise carried by the sailing vessels that plied the lake between the fort and Detroit. Nevertheless, it demanded the presence of an ensign or lieutenant with most of a company to stand guard over the valuable government and private wares deposited there. As commandant of Niagara, therefore, Caldwell found himself actually responsible for three forts and a vulnerable portage route some thirty miles long.

In theory, this British precinct at Niagara was administered by a civilian lieutenant governor, namely one Pierce Acton Sinnott. Sinnott was a Scotsman who had served in the crown's Southen Indian Department in the 1760's. He had assisted the Brit-

ish troops who ascended the Mississippi in 1765 to occupy the Illinois country, and he later acted as an assistant trade commissary in West Florida. He lost his job in a department staff reduction in 1768, however, and sailed for England the following spring. There he persuaded the secretary of state for American affairs that his services on the Mississippi had impaired his health. In compensation, he was granted an appointment (dated May 4, 1771) as lieutenant governor of Fortress Niagara with an annual salary of £150 to be paid from the North American military contingency fund. Sinnott held this office merely as a sinecure, however, and the American secretary directed the commander-in-chief to grant him a permanent leave of absence because of his supposed health problems. He faithfully collected his pay throughout the years of the American Revolution and possibly until his death in 1794, but he never

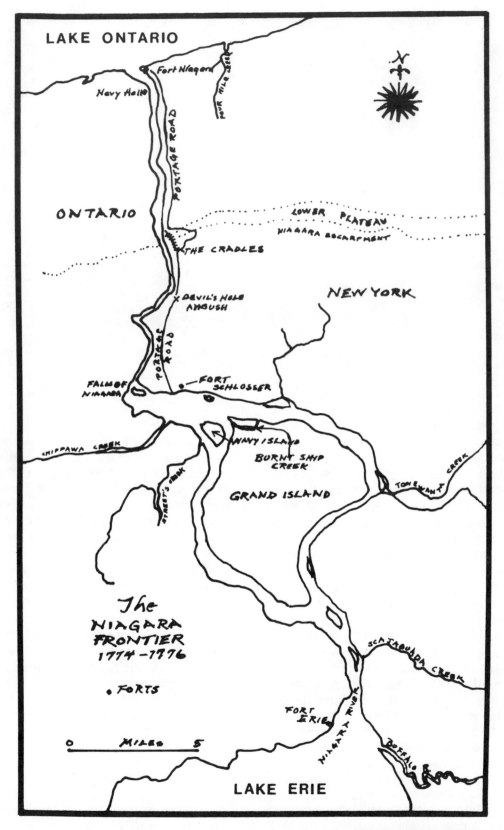

LAKE ONTARIO

Fort Niagara

Navy Hall

FOUR MILE CREEK

PORTAGE ROAD

ONTARIO

LOWER PLATEAU

NIAGARA ESCARPMENT

THE CRADLES

X DEVIL'S HOLE AMBUSH

NEW YORK

PORTAGE ROAD

FALLS OF NIAGARA

FORT SCHLOSSER

CHIPPAWA CREEK

NAVY ISLAND

BURNT SHIP CREEK

GRAND ISLAND

TONEWANT CREEK

STREET'S CREEK

The
NIAGARA
FRONTIER
1774-1776

• FORTS

SCATAQUARA CREEK

FORT ERIE

NIAGARA RIVER

BUFFALO

0 MILES 5

LAKE ERIE

Map by Marbud Prozeller.

16

REFE...
to
PICTURE
C.C — Cabins
D.DD — Line of Old French Tram way up the "3 mountains"
E — Great Gorge — cut through by the Falls
F.F — Niagara River —

The gorge cut by the Falls runs south and at right angle onto the mountain ridge

This mountain ridge runs east + west.

L A SALLE'S landing place Lewiston and line of Old FRENCH tram way up the "3 mountains"

The site of the Lower Landing and route of the "Cradles" were sketched by Lewiston artist James Van Cleve during the nineteenth century. He mistakenly attributed construction of the machine to the French. *Courtesy, William L. Clements Library.*

once left Britain to visit Niagara. His absence was no doubt a blessing for Colonel Caldwell, for he had a reputation as a "fractious and whimisical" man with a knack for making enemies.[22]

Without assistants or advisers of any kind, therefore, Caldwell was confronted with a formidable array of duties, which also encompassed areas far beyond the Niagara Frontier. Because Fort Niagara headquartered the regiment that garrisoned four of the five upper posts, it served as *de facto* capital of the British west. As the regiment's senior officer, Caldwell acted as commandant of Indian territory and the focus for all its military and government communications. Although Caldwell's supplies came from Quebec, his orders came from the commander-in-chief at New York City (while General Haldimand acted in that capacity) or at Boston (after General Gage returned from England in May, 1774). Sometimes Haldimand and Gage sent their instructions by ship to Quebec to be forwarded by the senior military officer or by Governor Carleton (who himself returned in September, 1774, from a sojourn in England), but they more often dispatched them by way of the New York fur traders' route through the Mohawk Valley and down the Onondaga River to Fort Ontario at Oswego, then abandoned except for a caretaker corporal's guard detached from Niagara. At the same time, the commander-in-chief's orders for the other outpost commandants usually passed first through Caldwell's hands, as did copies of their replies.

Thus, Caldwell oversaw the implementation of government policy throughout Indian territory, a duty which generated a continual flow of communications between him and his subordinate officers. So too did many

Fort Schlosser as rebuilt and enlarged in 1763. Although rather dilapidated by 1774, it was not substantially altered until 1779. *Courtesy, Public Record Office, W.O. 34, Jeffery Amherst Papers.*

local affairs at the various posts in the west, for the scattered King's officers depended upon one another's support. And, of course, Caldwell controlled all regimental matters, including the deployment of the troops among the posts and the orders regarding any operations they might undertake. Essentially unprepared by his military background for such diverse obligations, Caldwell was less awed by his responsibilities than by the sheer isolation of his situation. At Niagara, he confessed to his sister-in-law, he felt himself "cast away as I may justly term it upon the most desert part of this Continent."[23]

At Niagara, moreover, Caldwell came into daily contact with the continent's native people, and Indian diplomacy became one of his most important and time-consuming duties. A complete novice in the field of Indian affairs, however, he found himself "a stranger in this Indian World, and unacquainted with the business" of frontier statecraft.[24] Colonel Smith had given him a full report about the situation among the local tribes, but the government provided him with no assistant to offer informed counsel.[25] The military paid a blacksmith, Jacob Hansen (sometimes printed Harsin), to look after the Indians' needs at the post, but the Northern Superintendent of Indian Affairs, Sir William Johnson, had assigned to the three Niagara Frontier forts only a single interpreter, Jean-Baptiste De Couagne, a sickly and elderly *Canadien*.[26] The superintendent himself sent suggestions and information to the commandant by letter from Johnson Hall, his manor house and headquarters in the Mohawk Valley, and solicited intelligence from him, but for daily advice Caldwell probably depended heavily on the resident traders, particularly Edward Pollard. Pollard had come

Fort Erie stood on the very edge of Lake Erie. The vessel at anchor in this 1773 sketch by Ens. Henry De Berniere is probably the schooner *Dunmore. Courtesy, National Army Museum, London.*

out from England in 1760 and was by 1774 Niagara's leading merchant. He had intimate connections with the nearby Senecas and, moreover, acted as sutler, commissary, and financial agent for the British garrison. His responsibilities included furnishing the £ 100-200 worth of Indian presents that Niagara's commandant dispensed annually. These would be needed during Caldwell's frequent meetings with his two Indian neighbors, the Senecas and the Mississaugas.[27]

The Senecas were members of the Six Nations Confederacy (or League of the Iroquois), which also included the Mohawks, Oneidas, Onondagas, Cayugas, and Tuscaroras. The Senecas—Keepers of the Western Door of the Confederacy—dominated western New York. The most powerful and least Europeanized of the Six Nations, they had always been the least amenable of the Iroquois to British interests. In 1774 the Senecas seem to have numbered some 650-700 warriors, with a total population in the range of 2,600-3,000. Their settlements fell into two divisions: the Lower Senecas occupying the area from the shores of Seneca Lake westward to the upper Genesee River; and the Upper Senecas residing along the northern reaches of the Allegheny River. In the season of the fall hunt, the Senecas roamed the entire area west of Seneca Lake, moving down the Chemung River to the Susquehanna and down the Allegheny into eastern Ohio, where a band of expatriate Senecas and other Iroquois had established themselves as a separate group known as Mingoes.

With towns on the headwaters of the Ohio River and with relatives settled in the Ohio country, the Senecas considered themselves responsible for overseeing events among the Six Nations' western dependent and were considered a people of much consequence by the tribes of the midwest.

A group of Indians, probably of the Six Nations, at Niagara about 1783. Detail from "A View of Niagara taken from the Heights near Navy Hall" by James Peachey. *Courtesy, Public Archives of Canada, C-2035.*

Reputedly the most warlike of the Iroquois, Seneca warriors served as the strong western bulwark of the Confederacy. During Pontiac's uprising in 1763, Seneca warriors, acting without League approval, had attacked and massacred a British convoy of empty wagons along the Niagara portage as well as the redcoats who came to its rescue. At peace with the British since then, the Senecas regarded them as mere lessees of the Niagara riverbank, and Senecas frequently traveled from the Genesee and Allegheny villages to Niagara to trade and to keep a watchful eye on their tenants. Colonel Caldwell could regard them as friends but must treat them warily.[28]

Caldwell's western neighbors were the Mississaugas, a branch of the widespread Chippewa (or Ojibway) people. They had migrated from the upper Great Lakes during 1690-1710 and were firmly established in southern Ontario from Detroit to the eastern end of Lake Ontario by 1720. Nominal friends of the French, they had also allied themselves to the Six Nations and the British in 1746 and had developed close ties with the Senecas. They fought for the French during the French and Indian War but made peace with the British after the fall of Fort Niagara. Many small bands of Mississaugas lived along the streams flowing into northern Lake Ontario, but though they were a numerous people no reliable estimates of their population exist for this period. They rarely cultivated any land and subsisted by hunting and fishing, the products of which they regularly bartered at Oswegatchie and Niagara.[29]

Visited often by surrounding Indian peoples of such numbers and always uncertain loyalties and charged foremost with defending his king's post, Caldwell took stock of the fortifications and artillery at Niagara and his regiment's other garrisons as his first order of business. He found none of the 8th Regiment's forts too sturdy and fowarded this information to General Gage with a request for per-

An Iroquois longhouse. From Lewis Henry Morgan *League of the Ho-de'-no-sau-nee*, 1851.

mission to rebuild Niagara's firing platforms and some other wooden structures in the spring. In the meantime, he set about making short-term repairs, but he could do little more than keep pace with the steady deterioration worked on the fort's logs and sod by the region's ever-changing and often severe weather. He lacked sufficient workmen to accomplish more. With only three companies at Fort Niagara (the other being detached to Fort Schlosser and Erie under Lieutenant Samuel Willoe) plus six gunners from the Royal Regiment of Artillery, he had few men to spare from the daily routine of sentry, guard, and drill for fatigue parties. Moreover, Niagara had almost no civilians whom he might hire as part-time laborers. The best Caldwell could do was to stand on his guard, keep his regulars busy with axe, shovel, and hammer, and hope that trouble kept its distance.[30]

Shortly after his arrival, Caldwell did receive a few reinforcements. On September 6 Captain-Lieutenant Wil-

Ens. John Caldwell had his portrait painted in native dress he had collected at Detroit. *Courtesy, the King's Regiment Collection, National Museums and Galleries on Merseyside.*

liam Potts reached Niagara by way of Boston, New York, and Oswego with a party of thirteen recruits for the regiment. Of more immediate value than the untrained, unacclimated new soldiers was Potts himself, whom Caldwell regarded highly. Although the 8th most junior company-grade officer, Potts, who also acted as the regiment's quartermaster, had already served more than eighteen years as a regular officer, most of them on the American frontier. He had joined the Royal American Regiment as an ensign in 1756 and campaigned with it along the northern borders throughout the French and Indian War. After the fall of New France, he had been stationed at several wilderness posts, including Fort Pitt throughout the Indian siege of 1763 and prior to that, significantly, Fort Niagara. He had transferred to the 8th Regiment in 1765 when his own battalion was disbanded, and he could place considerable knowledge

Canise or "Great Sail", a Mississauga chief sketched by Elizabeth Simcoe in the 1790's. *Courtesy, Archives of Ontario.*

An Iroquois "gostoweh" or head dress. From Lewis Henry Morgan, *League of the Ho-de'-no-sau-nee*, 1851.

of the region and its peoples at Caldwell's disposal.[31]

Added responsibility for the colonel came with a second Niagara newcomer, his nephew and namesake, John Caldwell, the eldest son of Sir James and heir to the family baronetcy. Having just turned eighteen, young John had been sent to Quebec as a civilian volunteer in anticipation of his purchasing an army commission. Because Colonel Caldwell's brother Henry was preoccupied with his businesses and estates and because the colonel's friend and former commander, Lieutenant Colonel Richard Prescott of the 7th Regiment, had to leave Quebec for Boston, they shipped young John off to Fort Niagara. Obtaining there an ensigncy in the 8th, he came for awhile under the direct tutelage of the colonel, who assured Lady Caldwell that her son would have good companions in "the Gentlemen of the Regmnt., who are in every respect well bred, good natured, well disposed people & perfectly free from every Vice." Nevertheless, he lamented that young John had been exiled to a place as remote as Niagara, where his education must necessarily suffer.[32]

An accurate view of Niagara Falls drawn by Ens. Henry De Berniere in 1773. Lt. Col. Caldwell undoubtedly visited this well known natural wonder during his time at Fort Niagara. *Courtesy, National Army Museum, London.*

Echoes of Lord Dunmore's War

In the autumn of 1774 young John Caldwell's safety may have been of more immediate concern than his education to his uncle, for Colonel Caldwell had himself arrived at Niagara in the midst of the most serious troubles on the northern frontier in a decade. Avaricious Virginia land-seekers, determined to claim Kentucky lands west of the Indian boundary negotiated by Superintendent Sir William Johnson in 1768, had pushed the Ohio tribes into a conflict that would become known as Lord Dunmore's War. Border ruffians had instigated the violence in late April, 1774, by brutally murdering thirteen peaceable Mingoes, Shawnees, and Delawares in several incidents along the upper Ohio River. When male relatives of the Mingo and Shawnee victims sought justice through retaliatory raids, Virginia's frontier leaders screamed "savagery" and began to assemble their militia. A general Indian war, like that of 1763, seemed imminent. The imperial Northern Indian Department mobilized its agents to avert such a conflict or, failing that, to prevent the embattled Mingoes and Shawnees from gaining the support of the region's other tribes, particularly the Mingoes' relatives among the Six Nations.

The crown's agents managed to calm most Ohio tribesmen and their Indian neighbors, but during a major council with Six Nations leaders at Johnson Hall in mid-July Sir William Johnson had died suddenly, leaving Britain's Indian diplomacy in the hands of his nephew, Guy Johnson, the interim superintendent. The Six Nations chiefs did promise to assist the British peace efforts in the Ohio country, but they then retired to their central council place at Onondaga to evaluate their confederacy's place in this crisis. Meanwhile, further Virginian provocations early in August had destroyed the Shawnee's last hopes for re-establishing peace, and they resolved to fight to the bitter end. They dispatched couriers in every direction to beg other tribes to join them in their struggle. Three emissaries journeyed to Onondaga to offer the Shawnee war hatchet to the Six Nations. In this critical situation, with the Six Nations weighing their future actions and with many Seneca and Cayuga warriors eager to avenge their slain Mingo kinsmen, Colonel Caldwell obtained his on-the-job training in Indian diplomacy.[33]

Because the Seneca chiefs were engaged in other councils in mid-August, several weeks passed before Caldwell first met them. During that time he consulted the traders best acquainted with the Iroquois, and they predicted that the Six Nations would "remain upon a friendly footing." Nevertheless, during August and September Caldwell personally, as he informed General Gage, "spared neither trouble nor expence to find out the part the Six Nations were likely to take in these disputes" and "convered [conferred] with many of their chiefs & others, drunk & sober." At every meeting, he tried to convince the Seneca headmen of Iroquois weakness and of British strength, reminding them that since Britain had once conquered all America when at war with many other nations it could easily "now, when universal peace prevails, extirpate every savage upon the Continent." He told them he "was sent to Niagara in the character

Sir William Johnson. Portrait attributed to Matthew Pratt, c. 1772. *Courtesy, New York State Office of Parks, Recreation and Historic Preservation, Johnson Hall State Historic Site, Saratoga/Capital Region.*

of Sachem [civil chief], as well as Warrior" and promised them his assistance while their hatchet lay buried and eternal war if they should raise it.[34]

At Gage's request, Caldwell also gathered every scrap of intelligence he could obtain about Indian affairs. Much came from the Senecas he befriended, especially old Sciawa, a principal sachem of Genesee Castle, who was fond of the British and even fonder of their liquor. He fowarded these reports, particularly one concerning the anti-Britsh preachings of a *Canadien* trader living among the Allegheny Senecas, to both Gage and Guy Johnson. Because of the stories spread by such *Canadiens* and by the Shawnees and Mingoes, Caldwell learned, the Iroquois had been warmly debating for a year "whether or not they should strike the English" and their young men were "ripe as ever for michief." On the other hand, because he, Johnson, and other crown officials so assiduously supported the advocates of peace within the Confed-

eracy, he could report by late September that the warriors and war chiefs had agreed not only to consult with but also to obey their sachems, who, being old men with nothing to gain from war, naturally favored peace. Caldwell also learned from Sciawa that the Six Nations had refused the Shawnees' war hatchet, and he believed the sachems would keep their young men at home, provided the British could restore peace between the Virginians and the Ohio tribes.[35]

In the end, British officials were able to restrain the Indians but not the Virginians. Because of the efforts of Colonel Caldwell, Captain Lernoult at Detroit, Superintendent Johnson, and his agents at Pittsburgh, the Shawnees and Mingoes stood alone when John Murray, Earl of Dunmore, Virginia's royal governor, marched against them in October with two large militia armies. Heavily outnumbered, the Shawnees battled one of the militia columns to a standstill at Point Pleasant, but they failed to defeat it. When Lord Dunmore and the second column advanced to their towns along the Scioto River, the Shawnees sued for an armistice. Both sides accepted preliminary peace terms, which they agreed to ratify at a council at Pittsburgh the following spring. Infuriated by an attack on their villages by one of Dunmore's detachments, however, the Mingoes spurned the armistice and resolved to pursue an intermittant war of revenge against the Virginia backcountry. Although many among the Six Nations remained angered by the treatment of the Ohio tribes, British diplomacy that year had resulted in the League's commitment to maintaining peace with the colonial frontierspeople and in the emergence of its western viceroy, the important Allegheny Seneca chief Kayashuta, as the foremost proponent of peace in

Sir William Johnson died suddenly at his home, Johnson Hall, following an Indian council. Oil painting by Edward L. Henry. *Courtesy, Mr. John Knox, Piseco Lake, New York.*

the Ohio valley. By the end of October, Caldwell was able to assure his sister-in-law that the neighboring Indians seemed of friendly disposition "at present," just as Niagara's communications were about to be cut of "with all the world except the Savages."[36]

Colonel Caldwell was about to endure his first Niagara winter, which froze all water transport from December to May and smothered all land communication except for an occasional courier traveling by snowshoe. The political unrest then endemic in the east, fortunately, had not yet spread to the western posts. Although radical settlers in the Mohawk Valley had established a widely-supported committee of safety in Superintendent Johnson's own neighbhorhood, the traders who frequented Niagara from New York and Canada remained more interested in profits than politics. The colonel, therefore, still worried most about the temper of the Indians, wrote to Gage's military secretary in December that "our situation with them

being so very critical that it is impossible to say what part they will take next Spring." In these circumstances, he concluded, he dared not "deprive the Savages of any indulgence they have hitherto experienced." Because the Indians were dispersing for their winter hunt, however, he had little to do but to make preparations for the structural repairs he hoped to undertake in the spring, to represent General Gage's opinions to whatever tribesmen visited Niagara, and to ensure that Gage's orders reached the 8th's other garrisons. Gage based these orders on his perception that, "tho' our Affairs are not in the best Situation with the Savages, yet they are more peaceable above than we are in the lower parts of the Country." He dispatched his intial instructions regarding western policy to his post commanders by way of Guy Johnson in early October, and they certainly reached Niagara during November.

In these orders, directed to Caldwell, Lernoult, and De Peyster, Gage explained his wish that, if a general

25

Maj. Gen. Thomas Gage. *Courtesy, William L. Clements Library.*

Indian outbreak could not be avoided, the commandants convince the tribesmen to war only against the people who had injured them (meaning the Virginians) and not to attack the king's posts, whose troops had not harmed them and whose trade remained open to them. This altered somewhat the policy British officials had pursued throughout 1774 of promoting Indian friendship toward both British garrisons and British colonists. To ensure uniformity in his Indian policy at a time when British colonial policy lay in ruins, the commander-in-chief repeated his instructions at Christmastime to all his subordinates who had responsibilities in Indian diplomacy. Gage sent almost identical letters to northern and southern Indian superintendents Guy Johnson and John Stuart, Canadian military governor Guy Carleton, key post commanders Richard Lernoult and Hugh Lord, and western post commandant John Caldwell.

These letters reveal that Gage was then less concerned with protecting the colonists from Indians' anger than with ensuring King George of the Indians' friendship. To minimize the evil effects of the rash actions of one royal official (Dunmore), Gage reiterated, as he wrote Caldwell, that his representatives should "assure all the Nations, that the King highly disapproves of the Conduct of his Subjects towards them, and as a Proof of it they have seen None of the King's own Troops acting against them." The Indians must "be taught to look upon the King as their firm Friend," he explained most completely to Johnson, "and if they should Quarrel with any particular People, to Confine their Resentment to where the Provocation is given, and not begin Hostilities against the King's Troops or any People who have not injured them." Determined to employ every available means to retain the tribes' allegiance, he told Caldwell not only to "try to persuade them that it is their Interest not to quarrell with the King" but to warn them "if they molest the Posts all their Trade from below will be stopped." Realizing that his most dangerous military confrontations in the near future were likely to be colonial rather than native Americans, Gage was already contemplating the possibility of employing the Indians against the colonists, but he hinted at this only in his letter to Stuart.[37]

Gage's December orders reached Niagara in February, 1775, just in time for Caldwell to anounce the king's displeasure with the Virginians to the largest assemblage of Senecas to have gathered at the fort in some time. This news was, he reported, "received with great joy" by the old sachem Sciawa, the important war chief Adongot (Spruce-Carrier), and "all their suit," and by a chief and twenty-five warriors from the Allegheny, "formerly the worst disposed to us of all the Indians." Caldwell recognized that, while

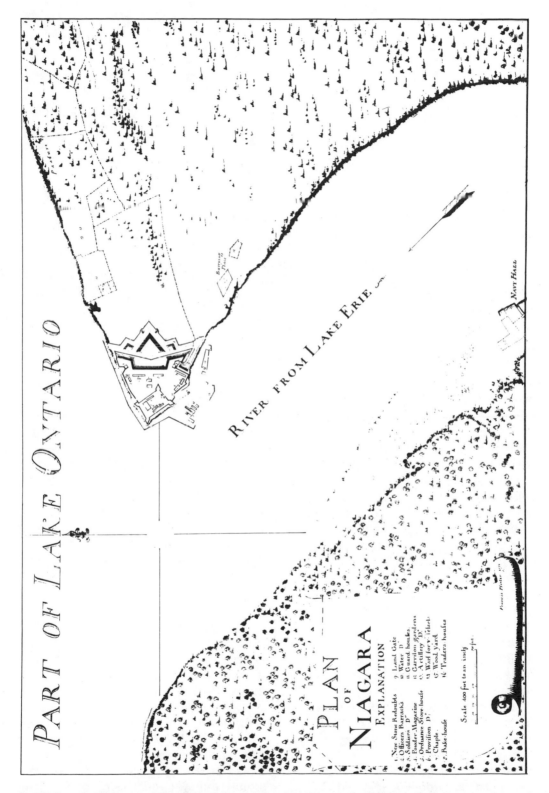

In 1771 Francis Pfister prepared a plan of the entire post of Niagara. In addition to the fort proper the garrison maintained pastures, extensive gardens and a cemetery near the river bank. Navy Hall is visible across the river. *Courtesy, William L. Clements Library.*

Untitled sketch of a dance showing Indians, soldiers and *Canadiens* attributed to Lt. John André, c. 1775. *Courtesy, William L. Clements Library.*

"every thing now bears the pacifick appearance," the Senecas' "great jealousy" over white encroachments along the Allegheny and the West Branch of the Susquehana would cause "ill blood" if the Shawnees ceded to the Virgnians any lands that the Senecas claimed. Moreover, he found that rumors of the British-colonial dispute had spread to all the Iroquois villages. The Senecas reported hearing stories "that His Majesty intended to deprive all his Colony of their lands, & then the Indians must loose theirs [and] that he had begun with the Bostonians." Caldwell endeavored to "undeceive" them and to convince them that their interests lay in retaining Britain's good graces. He found that

> ...*the old ones tho sensible of this, yet when in their cups & off their guard can not help saying that this long peace.will be the ruin of their nation, that their warriors are loosing their manhood & that their youth must become women, having no*

> *opportunities of exercising themselves in war, these are their real sentiments, which I am sure they will manifest when occasion offers with the least probability of success.*

The chief's unguarded remarks revealed a dilemma common to Indian society, in which the male filled three major roles—hunter, warrior, and statesman. Because the British had arranged a peace between the Iroquois and their old enemies among the southern tribes and because the British and their colonists had maintained peace with the Senecas since 1764, Seneca men had lacked an opportunity to learn or to practice their highly-valued military skills for a decade. Perhaps thinking they might revive their martial character as British allies, some Seneca headmen asked Caldwell "to look upon them as my warriors, ready to obey any orders I should give them." His professional eye judged them to be "fine active fellows, well armed, every-man his rifled Barrel gun, no bad alliance for the old steady veterans of the Kings Regmt." Writing to Gage in February, he gave his opinion that the Senecas "would not desire better sport than to attend your Excellency upon any expedition." He meant this merely as a comment upon the Senecas' apparent attitude rather than as a specific recommendation, for he still entertained hopes that political "tranquility" might be restored in the colonies by that coming summer. He little anticipated how soon Gage's army would be marching on expeditions. As he wrote, another letter was passing through Niagara in which a Schenectady merchant informed a friend at Detroit that in the Mohawk Valley, "Here is the Devil to Pay about Politicks and Liberty."[38]

Both Johnson and Gage realized that proselytizing by the Mohawk Valley's liberty boys might cost the

This portrait by Benjamin West has long been identified as Guy Johnson, nephew of Sir William and his successor as Superintendent of Indian Affairs. Although recent scholarship suggests that this likeness might actually have been intended to represent Sir William, it depicts the manner of dress affected by British Indian officers. Niagara Falls is shown in the left background. *Courtesy, National Gallery of Art, Washington, D.C.*

A warrior of the Six Nations. *Drawing by Joe Lee.*

crown its traditional alliance with the Six Nations, and Johnson labored throughout the early months of 1775 to assure the Iroquois that their interests lay with the British. To guide his dealings with the Indians, Gage sent during February and March instructions based on the simple directive: "You are to tell them the King is their Friend, and expects them to be his." Johnson was to remind the Iroquois that the crown, not the colonists, had provided past favors and controlled future commerce. Finally, Guy was to tell them the king's troops would never molest them while they chose to remain the king's friends, "but on the Contrary, that they may expect from him every assistance and Jus-

The South Redoubt at Fort Niagara was constructed in 1770, and followed a year later by the similar North Redoubt.

Gage's communications with Johnson and Johnson's with Caldwell remained yet unimpeded by anything but the weather, and Caldwell seems to have received his superior's latest orders during April. The colonel believed that he had succeeded in carrying out Gage's wishes during early 1775 and "in keeping my Neighbouring Indians in good Humour." He felt he had convinced Seneca leaders that their people would benefit from Britain's favor but would suffer terribly from Britain's power "if by the least injury to His Majesty's (not the Colonys) Troops they incurred our displeasure." Nevertheless, the Six Nations also held the crown accountable for two provocations by Britain's unruly colonists. First, they still worried that the Virginians would coerce land cessions from the Shawnees at the approaching Pittsburgh council. And, secondly, they expressed discontent during the winter over the increasing scarcity and high price of the gunpowder so indispensable for their hunting, a situation caused largely by the colonists' politically-motivated nonimportation of merchandise from Britain. Caldwell could do nothing to influence the negotiations at Pittsburgh, but he knew that the Iroquois might be supplied with European merchandise by way of Canada once winter released its grip on Lake Ontario and the St. Lawrence. The first warm breezes of summer, however, brought instead alarming news of insurrection and war throughout the colonies.[40]

tice he can give them."

As Gage had done previously he coordinated his instructions to Johnson with his post commanders. He wrote to Caldwell on March 4, directing him "to do all in your power to keep the Indians in good humour and to assure them on all Occasions of the Kings friendship for them." Caldwell was to tell the tribesmen that, even if they went to war, they might still receive supplies at the posts if they warred only against those who provoked them and not against British troops. Actually, Gage was still following the policy he had formulated in October, 1774. The commander-in-chief was not yet ready to draw the northern tribes into the British-colonial crisis or to encourage frontier conflict to divert his potential colonial

A Distant Rebellion

Following Lieutenant Colonel Francis Smith's disastrous march to and from Concord on April 19, 1775, General Gage found Boston surrounded by a rapidly growing host of New England militia and the eastern colonies risen in armed rebellion. Guy Johnson learned of this when visiting New York City late in April, and he hurried back to his manor, Guy Park, to counter the activities of the New York rebels, who began then to interfere openly in his dealings with the Six Nations. For a month he engaged in an escalating skirmish of threats and gestures with Mohawk Valley and Albany committeemen, but he finally realized that he would be unable to hold an upcoming general council with the Iroquois at his home as planned. Sometime between May 25 and 30, while he was preparing to relocate his office into Iroquois country where he might confer with the chiefs undisturbed, John Stedman (the Niagara portage concessionaire) reached Guy Park from Boston bearing secret instructions from Gage for the superintendent and for Colonel Caldwell.[41]

In letters dated May 10 Gage reported briefly that "A Rebellion is broke out in this Province" and that communications with his western officials had become nearly impossible "as the Posts are stopped, and every person thro' the Country searched." Only Stedman's opportune journey back to Niagara allowed Gage to inform them of his own predicament and to relay intelligence that "the Rebels intend attacking Ticonderoga," the Lake Champlain fortress held by only one company of the 26th Regiment of Foot. Up to this point, Gage had not called upon any of his officers

to engage Indians in the king's service. But he knew that his own besieged army could render no assistance to the threatened caretaker garrisons at Ticonderoga and nearby Crown Point (which had both actually fallen on May 10 to a force of Green Mountain Boys) or reinforce the two regiments (the 7th and 26th) Governor Carleton then had in Laurentian Canada. Therefore, he orderd Johnson to inform Carleton of the situation at Boston and the threat to Ticonderoga and Crown Point and "to concert with him the Assembling of the Indians and the proper means to be taken for the support of that part of the Country [the Champlain frontier]." In a similar letter, Gage asked Caldwell to cooperate with Johnson and Carleton. He freed the Niagara

Lt. Col. Francis Smith of the 10th Regiment of Foot passed command of Niagara to Caldwell in 1774. The following year Smith led British troops from Boston to raid the villages of Lexington and Concord. *Courtesy, National Army Museum, London.*

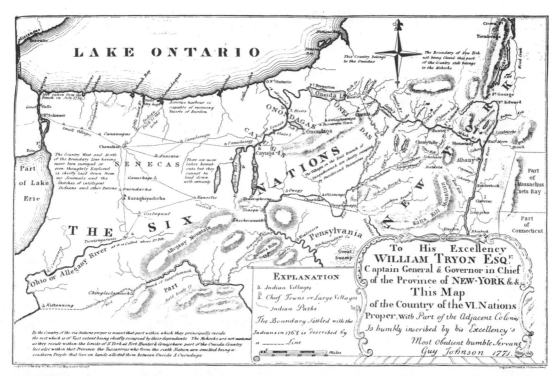

Guy Johnson's map of the New York frontier was published in 1771. This nineteenth century copy was printed in *Documentary History of New York*, IV, 660.

commandant "Hereafter [to] act from the Intelligence you get as your prudence directs you." He ordered him, however, to ready the warriors of the Six Nations to assist whatever operations Carleton undertook. Specifically, he wrote,

> I would have you immediately cultivate the friendship of the Indians as much as possible. Have them ready to detach on the first notice and in the mean time have scouts out to get what Intelligence you can. It is said the Rebels intend attacking Ticonderoga, if so, a body of Indians may be of great use there, and to act with the 7th Regiment (ordered there) on the Frontiers of this Province [Massachusetts]. Coll. Johnson will give you all the Assistance he can with the Indians, and likewise what Intelligence he can gather.[42]

In the months after Lexington and Concord, Gage several times encouraged Carleton to distract Boston's rebel besiegers by a show of force on Massachusetts' western frontiers. On April 27, for instance, he had urged the Quebec governor to send the 7th Regiment and Canadian volunteers to Crown Point to "make some diversion." It was to assist this enterprise and protect its base that Gage ordered Johnson and Caldwell to engage Indian warriors. For lack of an immediate post to Quebec, he directed Johnson to forward this latest information to Carleton. Before the next vessel sailed from Boston for the St. Lawrence he heard that the rebels had captured Ticonderoga and harbored designs against Niagara, Detroit, and the abandoned fort at Oswego, and he also received Caldwell's February letter indicating the Senecas' ostensible willingness to join the king's troops.

In shipborne dispatches on May 20, therefore, Gage ordered Carleton to

Guy Johnson abandoned his home, Guy Park, in the spring of 1775. *Courtesy, New York State Office of Parks, Recreation and Historic Preservation, Guy Park State Historic Site, Saratoga/Capital Region.*

take immediate command of all military matters in Canada and of all the frontier posts in the northern district. He enclosed letters (open for Carleton's inspection) to be forwarded to Caldwell, Lernoult, and De Peyster, directing them to the Canadian governor-general for future orders and financial warrants. The rebellion of every colony but Quebec, he wrote, required Caldwell "to engage all the Indians you possibly can, in the King's interest" to cooperate with Carleton. Nonetheless, Gage did not order Lernoult and De Peyster to recruit the western tribes but merely to cultivate their friendship "as they may be wanted for His Majesty's Service" These orders did not reach Carleton until mid-June and could not have reached Caldwell before the end of that month.[43]

Gage's plan for using regulars, Canadians, and Indians to relieve the pressure on Boston was never implemented however, because the rapid spread of the rebellion disrupted both the imperial Northern Indian Department and the royal government of Quebec and because the Six Nations, so recently resolved upon a policy of peace, declined to get involved in an armed conflict. Because of his weak situation at Niagara, Colonel Caldwell could also contribute little to Gage's scheme. About mid-June Stedman delivered Gage's May 10 instructions placing the colonel on his own to protect his post and cooperate with Johnson and Carleton as he judged best. Probably not many days later he also received a dispatch from Carleton informing the upper post commanders that rebels had captured Ticonderoga and Crown Point and then crossed the border to raid into Quebec Province. Carleton warned the King's officers "to be upon their Guard," and Caldwell undoubtedly added his own caveat when he fowarded this news to Lernoult and De Peyster. What special steps he took to strengthen Niagara's forts and place their garrisons on alert are not known, but he did manage to assist Johnson in a limited manner.

Guy Johnson departed his beloved Guy Park on May 31 when his family and an armed entourage of some 90 Mohawks and 120 whites, comprising friends, tenants, and the entire staff of his Indian Department (including his kinsmen and deputies Daniel Claus and John Dease, secretary Jo-

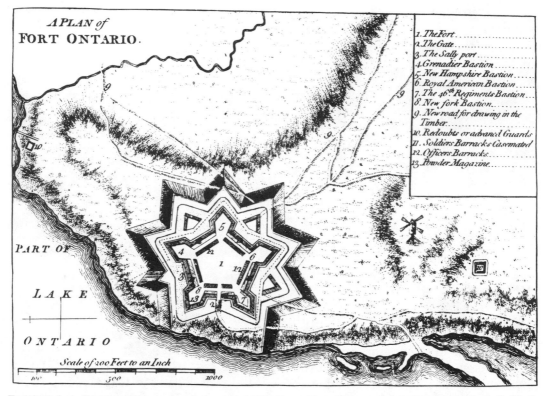

A PLAN of
FORT ONTARIO.

1. The Fort
2. The Gate
3. The Sally port
4. Grenadier Bastion
5. New Hampshire Bastion
6. Royal American Bastion
7. The 46th Regiments Bastion
8. New York Bastion
9. New road for drawing in the Timber
10. Redoubts or advanced Guards
11. Soldiers Barracks Casemated
12. Officers Barracks
13. Powder Magazine

PART OF
LAKE
ONTARIO

Scale of 200 Feet to an Inch

Fort Ontario as it appeared upon completion about 1760. From Mary Rocque, *A Set of Plans and Forts in North America ...*, 1763. *Courtesy, William L. Clements Library.*

seph Chew, and interpreters John Butler and Joseph Brant). By June 8 his party was safely encamped at deserted, dilapidated Fort Stanwix at the head of navigation on the Mohawk River. Although some Oneidas and other Iroquois met him there, he could not convene his council because he had not carried sufficient supplies with him and could no longer obtain any from New York. He therefore appealed for aid to the only accessible crown officials. From Fort Stanwix he wrote to Carleton at Montreal, asking the governor to send provisions, ammunition, Indian presents, and two hundred troops. He also dispatched letters to Captain Forster at Oswegatchie and Colonel Caldwell at Niagara, requesting that they send vessels and provisions to meet him at old Fort Ontario at Oswego.

All three officers responded as best they could to meet Johnson's needs,

although the great distance retarded somewhat the arrival of Carleton's cargo of Indian goods. Moreover, the governor could not supply even two redcoats, let alone two hundred. Having received Johnson's message after only a few days, however, Caldwell acted quickly. He loaded the sixty-ton sloop *Charity* with ninety barrels of dried and salted foodstuffs (all his storehouses could spare) and a quantity of arms and sent her to Oswego with a few soldiers and a small delegation of Wyandots who had come from Detroit to attend Johnson's council. The vessel anchored off Fort Ontario only a few days after Johnson's party arrived on June 17, and its cargo and passengers helped the superintendent carry on a moderately successful conference with nearly 1,500 Indians representing all members of the League of the Iroquois. Finding the Six Nations friendly to the crown but firmly neutral in the British-colonial conflict, Johnson embarked his white followers and a deputation of a hundred or so Iroquois on Caldwell's sloop and several bateaux and set sail for Montreal on July 11 to confer with Carleton. His departure left Caldwell the sole royal authority anywhere on the New York frontier.

The colonel must have finally received Gage's May 20 orders, which placed him and the other western commandants under Carleton's direct command, about the first of July. The trade route from Albany and Schenectady and hence Caldwell's communications with the Mohawk Valley also remained open at that time, and he was able to begin discreet exchange of messages with Sir John Johnson (the late superintendent's son and the interim superintendent's cousin), who had remained at Johnson Hall to protect his estates and coordinate loyalist activities in the Valley. From friendly merchants in the Valley, Caldwell received the latest New York newspapers and rumors that rebel troops had designs on Stanwix, Oswego, and the shipping at Oswegatchie. Like the other post commandants, Caldwell reacted to such news of rebel military success and intentions with what might be termed the "Ticonderoga syndrome," a real fear the he too might easily suffer the disgrace and professional ruin of having a colonial rabble overrun the rotting, undermanned forts for which he was responsible.

Consequently, Caldwell's overriding priority became the defense of Niagara by every available means. Upon receiving Gage's first wartime orders, he had written to Carleton, the governor reported on June 28, complaining "of his garrison being too weak for all the Services it has to perform" and apprehending "the Virginians [at Pittsburgh] making an attempt upon Fort Erie, and endeavouring to destroy the King's Vessels." With only two hundred or so King's regulars to protect three separate forts, a thirty-mile portage, and weakly-manned ships on two lakes,

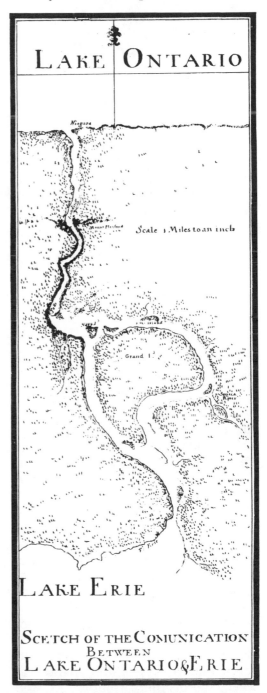

"Scetch of the Communication Between Lake Ontario & Erie" by Lt. Francis Pfister, 1773. The defense of this vulnerable, thirty-mile waterway and portage was one of Lt. Col. Caldwell's chief concerns. *Courtesy, British Library, Crown Maps, cxxi, 76.*

The gunners of Fort Niagara's Royal Artillery detachment were not, under normal circumstances, required to stand guard or perform fatigue duties. *Drawing by Joe Lee.*

therefore, Caldwell simply dared not send detachments of troops and Indians anywhere.[44] In fact, circumstantial evidence indicates that he may have transferred one of Captain Lernoult's companies to Niagara after learning of the colonial rebellion, sending it back to winter at Detroit only after its musketmen had helped guard the colonel's forts during the vulnerable months of summer and autumn.[45]

While Caldwell's redcoats stood watch on Niagara's rickety parapets that summer, the British cause suffered one reverse after another all along the northern frontier. At Montreal Johnson and his deputies managed to win Canada's wavering mission tribesmen back to the British

cause, but Johnson and Carleton squabbled angrily over matters of authority and Indian policy. Meanwhile, a congressional army based at Ticonderoga mounted an invasion of Quebec Province, and when the rebels threatened Montreal in October Johnson and his retinue fled to England. Johnson left British-Indian relations in shambles in Canada and in New York.

After meeting Johnson at Oswego, Six Nations leaders had retired to Onondaga and decided that their confederacy should follow a policy of armed neutrality in the white people's civil war. They opened negotiations with the Indian commissioners appointed by Congress and affirmed Iroquois neutrality and friendship for the colonists at a major council at Albany in early September. On the Six Nations' southwestern border, the rebels had established a committee of safety at Pittsburgh in May and effectively neutralized both Johnson's deputy there, Alexander McKee, and Governor Dunmore's agent, John Connolly. Thereafter, rebel officials supervised dealings with the Ohio tribes and the Allegheny Senecas. Throughout the summer of 1775, therefore, Britain's relations with the Six Nations were left largely in the inexperienced hands of the King's colonel at Niagara.[46]

During these months Caldwell conducted his own intensive diplomacy with the western tribes of the Six Nations, but he never did succeed in enlisting their warriors as Gage had wished. He sent out invitations that, supplemented by recommendations Johnson had made at Oswego, drew a number of the Lower and Upper Senecas to Fort Niagara in late August and early September. After the Onondaga Council settled upon its policy of neutrality, moreover, the Six Nations not only sent deputies to confer with the rebels at Albany but simultaneously sent other envoys "to Niagara to inform the Kings Officers & to strengthen our Friendship with them." Although Caldwell neither spent a great deal more on the Indians than usual nor persuaded them to abandon their league's strategy during his generally amicable meetings with them, he did introduce strong arguments to the effect that Six Nations welfare, even survival, lay clearly in adherence to the British cause.

Caldwell made three specific points, particularly directing his comments to the Senecas of the Allegheny who still suspected the intentions and watched the actions of the Virginians at Pittsburgh. As repeated at Pittsburgh by a talkative Mohawk, the colonel first told the Senecas that he knew they would soon be called to a treaty at Fort Pitt "but that they ought not to go to it nor regard anything the Bigknife [Virginians] might say to them for tho he had a very smooth Oily Tongue his heart was not good." Secondly, he advised the Iroquois that only the British could supply the manufactured goods the Indians required. The colonists' war against King George deprived them of their only source of gunpowder and clothing, Caldwell told his visitors, but if the Six Nations "would keep hold of the Chain of Friendship which their [British] Father put into their hands, they would not want." He backed his words with "a Keg of Powder & Lead in Proportion, and some Goods." Finally, hoping to preclude any attempt by the rebels to march against his post, he offered the Indians military assistance if the colonists tried to enter Indian territory. He asked them to watch the actions of the Big Knives closely, to send headmen to warn them off should they cross the Ohio, and to send to him for support if the Virginians refused to retire. He promised to order off the colonists himself, and "if they would

A sloop of the Naval Department from a watercolor of Fort Niagara, c. 1784. This vessel might be *Caldwell*.

not pay any regard to what he said he would gather all his People and fight them." In this, he argued, the British and Indians shared a common interest. "It might happen," he said, "that he might be thrown down in the Struggle but if he fell they must fall with him for the Big Knife had been pushing them back for a long time and would not rest till he had got all this Country." Indeed, he declared, "he and they were so linked together they would be never Separated but must stand or fall together." These were words that the Senecas would ponder for months to come.[47]

Caldwell's words, spoken at a critical time when the Iroquois well knew of Britain's many troubles in America, proved both perceptive and persuasive. He might have received written suggestions from Guy Johnson, and he certainly had listened to the advice of canny traders like Edward Pollard and knowledgeable officers like Captain William Potts. Of more importance he had learned quickly the intricacies of Indian diplomacy, and his dealings with the Iroquois served to strengthen British ties with the Six Nations in the long run.

For the short run, the colonel concentrated on defensive preparations through construction and intelligence-gathering. He put his entire

When armed rebellion cut off Niagara from British headquarters in Boston, Lt. Col. Caldwell's correspondence was directed to Quebec Governor Guy Carleton. *Courtesy, Public Archives of Canada, C-2833.*

garrison to work cutting trees in the woods and repairing or replacing the decayed timber in the fortifications. He even insisted upon the assistance of Niagara's artillery detachment over the protests of its commander, Lieutenant Henry Du Vernet, who objected that his six gunners were not required to perform such fatigue duties. Caldwell might also have been able to call upon the services of an addition to the crown's Lake Ontario fleet. Evidently sometime during the summer or autumn of 1775 the Navy Hall shipwrights completed and launched one of the vessels the British had begun in 1774. They fitted this thirty-ton sloop with two small cannons and named her *Caldwell*.[48]

Colonel Caldwell also endeavored to preserve his tenuous land links through Six Nations territory to loyalists and other sources of information in eastern New York. Pollard's commercial correspondence with the Mohawk Valley remained uninterrupted at least until the end of the year, and a few New York traders managed to journey westward to Ni-

agara and Detroit with their cargoes, albeit under the scrutiny of the Albany, Schenectady, and Mohawk Valley committees of safety. By Iroquois runners who used John Thompson's homestead (the westernmost in the Mohawk Valley) as a way station, Caldwell also exchanged messages and intelligence with Sir John Johnson, who had become the Valley's last bulwark of support for the king.[49]

Throughout the summer and autumn of 1775, Caldwell seems to have acted largely on his own initiative and to have received few, if any, meaningful instructions from his new superior, General Carleton, who formally became British military commander-in-chief for the northern district in October when Gage was replaced as commander-in-chief at Boston by Lieutenant General William Howe. Carleton was much too preoccupied with his own increasingly ineffective efforts to fend off General Richard Montgomery's invading army to worry much about the problems of his officers in the distant interior. Furthermore Carleton exhibited great ambiguity in dealing with the Indians. Although he advocated using every available method to coax or even coerce the often reluctant northern tribes into declaring their loyalty to the crown and also their willingness to serve its cause, he—unlike Gage and Johnson—was averse actually to employ Indians in any serious military capacity. Consequently, his infrequent references to Indian affairs in his letters to the upper posts during this period rarely directed the commandants to do anything more than foster the Indians' goodwill. As Caldwell approached his second winter at Niagara, however, the arrivals of two officials from Montreal heralded significant changes in his status as military commander of Indian territory and as Britain's principal spokesman to the Six Nations.

Revolutionary Change Touches Niagara

As late as September, 1775, the King's officers at Fort Niagara were able to send off to their superiors in England dispatches that could still pass safely through Montreal to the ships departing Quebec and finally reach London about Christmastime. Colonel Caldwell wrote to General Bigoe Armstrong, the 8th colonel-in-chief, apparently about internal regimental matters. His adjutant, Captain James Webb, who also acted as his regiment's deputy commissary of musters, assembled and prepared the financial accounts of the sundry companies and several officers and submitted them to the regiment's London agent, Edmund Armstrong, a half-pay captain and close relative of the general's. Neither Caldwell nor Webb, however, seems to have reported anything out of the ordinary at Niagara.[50]

Despite the reported threat posed by the colonial insurrectionists, the warfare of the American Revolution had not yet actually come home to the defenders of the Niagara Frontier. A more immediate danger to Niagara, however, arose from the rebel army that invaded Laurentian Canada that September, impairing Caldwell's communications, endangering his logistic lifeline, and engaging the attention of the colonel's immediate superior, Quebec's governor-general, Guy Carleton. Although the beleaguered governor neglected to send Caldwell orders regarding the role of the upper posts in the Revolutionary conflict, two refugees from the fighting near Montreal brought Caldwell news that changed his own responsibilities in the British west.

Henry Hamilton (a former captain in the 15th Regiment of Foot) stopped

Detroit's Lt. Gov. Henry Hamilton. *Courtesy, The Harvard University Portrait Collection.*

at Fort Niagara in mid-October while en route to his new office as lieutenant governor of Detroit. He had departed Montreal hastily on Carleton's order as General Richard Montgomery's rebel army closed around St. Johns and Chambly, the British posts on the Richelieu River, late in September. Hamilton apparently brought no new instructions from the governor, but he was able to inform the colonel of the seriousness of the military situation along the St. Lawrence and of a new system of governance that was taking effect in the British west. Hamilton was the first to arrive of the civil administrators who would henceforth govern the upper posts under the provisions of the Quebec Act of 1774, which had become effective May 1, 1775.[51]

Owing much to Carleton's persistent personal efforts when in England, the Quebec Act established a

Detail of Fort Niagara from James Peachey's "A View of Niagara taken from the Heights near Navy Hall". The traders' houses in "the Bottoms" are visible at water level behind the snow-rigged vessel. The buildings to the right of the ship were constructed during the War for Independence for use by the Indian Department. *Courtesy, Public Archives of Canada, C-2035.*

new provincial government for Quebec with powers vested in a crown-appointed governor (Carleton) and legislative council. It also extended provincial jurisdiction to the western lands formerly claimed by New France. Quebec's boundary was expanded southwestward up the St. Lawrence, through Lake Ontario and the Niagara River to Lake Erie, along the western edge of Pennsylvania to the Ohio River, down the Ohio to the Mississippi, and northward to the height of land separating the Great Lakes from Hudson Bay. This simple expedient provided civil government for the *Canadien* settlements in Indian territory and placed every major Indian tribe in the north except the Six Nations within Quebec's administrative charge.[52]

Although Carleton had lobbied to have Fort Niagara included within his enlarged province, the ministry had excluded it because of the competing claims of both New York and the Six Nations.[53] Oswegatchie still lay outside Quebec's bounds also, but the other posts, including Fort Erie, for which Caldwell or his officers had military responsibility now lay within the Province of Quebec. According to the crown's instructions, Carleton was to establish in the remote parts of

the province five subsidiary governments, to be centered at Gaspé, Vincennes, Kaskaskia, Michilimackinac, and Detroit. To each the ministry appointed a lieutenant governor who would assume all civil duties previously handled by garrison commanders, including Indian diplomacy and trade, but the ranking officer at each post would retain complete control of the regular troops stationed there. Neither the ministry nor the governor, however, delineated the exact authority of and relationship between the senior civil and military officials who were thereafter to coexist at Detroit, Michilimackinac, and Kaskaskia.

The ambiguity of this arrangement portended rivalry and dissension in years to follow, but for the time being this new organization affected Caldwell minimally. He had no authority over the lieutenant governors and consequently lost some of his previous influence over affairs at some other posts, but he continued to supervise the curtailed activities of the other garrison commanders as their regimental superior. Governor Carleton and his civil subordinates also gained responsibility for the naval department, but Caldwell retained his authority to control ship movements on the Great Lakes. As commandant of Niagara, he remained subject to the orders of Carleton as commander-in-chief. Because of the rebellion in the east, only Hamilton of the lieutenant governors was able to make his way to his new government in 1775, and Caldwell could trust Captain Lernoult (a thoroughly responsible officer) to work out his own accommodation with Detroit's new civil administrator.[54]

On November 17, a month after Hamilton stopped over, John Butler arrived at Niagara with a party from Guy Johnson's Indian Department. Just before leaving Montreal for England, Johnson had obtained Carleton's permission for some of his recently-appointed "officers &c to winter in the Indian Country," and he persuaded interpreter Butler to go to Niagara as his agent to deal with the Six Nations. Butler agreed to accept this assignment only after Johnson promised to recommend him to the ministry for a future deputyship in his department. For the interim, Johnson gave him on October 10 an appointment as "Assistant Agent and Resident at Niagara during pleasure" and a set of written instructins. To assist Butler, he sent with him Lieutenants Nathaniel Hillyer, Daniel Steel, and James Bennet, and four rangers, and he also directed Lieutenants John and William Johnston to winter among the Senecas, with whom these brothers had traded for many years. Officers and rangers alike were to be subject to Butler's orders. He set up Indian Department headquarters in a house in the traders' quarter between the fort and the river and immediately set about carrying out the Indian policy of his superiors.[55]

Caldwell considered Butler a welcome addition to his staff and gave him every assistance in executing his mission to the Iroquois. While Butler

The only known likeness of John Butler is a posthumous oil painting on board done by Henry Oakley in 1834. *Courtesy, Niagara Historical Society, Niagara-on-the-Lake, Ontario.*

relieved the colonel of the onerous details of Indian diplomacy, the agent actually served two other masters, officials whose rivalry placed him in an unenviable position. Butler considered himself responsible first to Johnson and bound by the written instructions—sadly no longer extant—given him by the superintendent and by any future orders he might find means to send. Nevertheless, Butler also felt obliged to follow Carleton's wishes in Indian matters and even asserted later that it was the governor who had ordered him to Niagara. In point of fact, Carleton's military authority over Niagara meant that he also controlled Butler's supply of money and Indian presents. Because Carleton and Johnson disagreed vehemently over Indian policy—the former opposing and the latter urging the use of war parties against the rebels—Butler's dual allegiance would complicate his efforts

By 1775 "taking up the hatchet" had become a common frontier euphemism for a declaration of war by native warriors. From Lewis Henry Morgan, *League of the Ho-de'-no-sau-nee*, 1851.

considerably after Johnson returned to New York City in 1776 and began to issue orders that contradicted Carleton's. In November, 1775, however, neither Johnson nor Carleton could supervise his activities effectively. Montreal had fallen to Montgomery on November 13, and by mid-month Johnson was sailing eastward across the Atlantic and Carleton was besieged in Quebec City. It did not take long for news of British disasters to circulate among the Six Nations, and modifying that confederacy's declared neutrality became Butler's great challenge.

Butler considered his mission as encompassing goals far less ambitious than Gage's and Johnson's wish that royal agents induce the Indians to take up the British hatchet. More realistic than they, Butler agreed with Carleton that "the part that the Indians would take was at that time very doubtful." At Niagara he learned from Caldwell that "many Rebel emissaries" had gone among the Six Nations during Johnson's absence and succeeded all too well in seducing them "from their attachment to the King," especially by reports of the successful invasion of Canada. Therefore, regardless of the contents of Johnson's written instructions, Butler determined that only the directions Carleton had also given him provided a practical course of action. And, as he later remembered, Carleton's "expectations at that period went no farther than to keep them

in a State of *Neutrality.*" Consequently, for the immediate future Butler would strive to win the entire Iroquois confederacy back into the king's camp, but he would refrain from urging the Indians to go to war.[56]

Caldwell had gained in Butler an associate eminently qualified to match the Six Nations headmen in frontier statecraft. He had traded, warred, and politicked with the Iroquois for twenty years as a representative and friend of the late Sir William Johnson. Moreover, his knowledge of Indian languages included Seneca, which permitted him to deal confidentially with the leaders of that nation.[57] Butler also affiliated himself with Niagara's existing commercial power structure by selecting a natural ally, Edward Pollard, as his chief though unofficial assistant. Both were self-made frontier entrepreneurs who shared experience and expertise in the Indian trade.

Because Pollard, one of Niagara's principal merchants, had been the garrison's sutler, commissary, financial agent, and supplier of Indian presents for some years, Butler arranged for him to perform the same duties for the Indian Department and also to care for all its affairs whenever diplomacy or other business took the agent to Indian country or Montreal. Butler and Pollard may also have collaborated in a mercantile partnership in order to profit privately from their public duties, but the evidence on this point is sketchy, unreliable, and not entirely convincing. Pollard explained his role at Niagara as "having the first three years of the rebellion the sole supplying & a principle share of superintending the Indians." Both he and Butler comprehended that maintaining a reliable source of European manufactures, whether from public or private storehouse, was Britain's best means of regaining the Six Nations' dependence on the crown and thereby reaffirming their loyalty.

At about the time of Butler's arrival a convoy of bateaux also reached Niagara bearing a great quantity of trade goods that merchants had dispatched from Montreal shortly before the town capitulated. The military turmoil, however, seems to have disrupted the normal late-season shipments of crown cargoes to the western posts. Moreover, the rebel occupation of the St. Lawrence Valley thereafter cut off Niagara from its source of all supplies, provisions as well as merchandise, the direst situation possible for merchant Pollard, ambassador Butler, and soldier Caldwell.[58]

Butler's presence somewhat eased Caldwell's fears about a possible Indian threat to his garrison, but at the same time the threat from the rebels was increasing ominously. After Montgomery had taken Montreal, in fact, he had suggested that Niagara's stores of gunpowder made it a worthy objective for Congress's armies. Caldwell was well aware of the dangers posed by rebel forces in Canada and New York, for he learned of the fall of St. Johns and Montreal, the siege of Quebec, and the obstruction of his supply routes from the last travelers from Canada and from the letters and colonial newspapers sent by Pollard's mercantile connections in New York. Among the last messages from the St. Lawrence, however, there evidently came none of significance from General Carleton. Even though Lieutenant Andrew Parke of the King's Regiment left Montreal on November 2 to join Captain Forster at Oswegatchie, the events of the ensuing eight months indicate that Carleton entrusted neither him nor anyone else with instructions for the upper post commanders to engage in military action or Indian diplomacy that might assist the

ONE OF THE STONE REDOUBT'S at Niagara built 1770.
Scale 16 feet to an inch

The South Redoubt, constructed in 1770, was one of the strongest parts of Niagara's fortifications. Drawing by Lt. Francis Pfister, 1773. *Courtesy, British Library, Crown Maps, cxxi, 76.*

embattled royal forces in Laurentian Canada. Rather, as Gage once had, he left Caldwell to meet the crisis according to his own best judgment.[59]

The colonel seems to have exercised his authority to the fullest extent possible to maintain the commercial atmosphere most conducive to Butler's dealings with the Indians. He certainly established a close working relationship with John Stedman, and he supported the concessionaire's measures for operating the portage, sometimes in the face of merchants' complains about Stedman's charges and strict system of weights and measures. Caldwell displayed equal firmness with the traders when the *Chippawa,* a private sloop of fifty tons burden, was wrecked on the beach near Presque Isle (present Erie, Pennsylvania) on November 26 while making one last run from Fort Erie to Detroit with trade goods. The crew managed to get ashore and off-load part of the cargo, but the sailors had few provisions and were soon surrounded by large numbers of Indians anxious to get at the ship's many kegs of rum.

Presbyterian minister Samuel Kirkland exercised considerable influence over his flock of Oneidas and Tuscaroras. *Courtesy, Hamilton College, Clinton, NY.*

Learning of the *Chippawa's* fate on December 7, Caldwell feared that the rum might occasion altercations between the crewmen and the Indians or that rebels from Pittsburgh might seize the sloop's militarily-valuable cargo. When he sent a rescue party to Presque Isle with a small boat, therefore, he ordered the ship's master to abandon the wreck site and to destroy all the merchandise (even though privately owned) he could not carry back with him to Fort Erie. He wished at any cost "to avoid all disputes with the Savages" and to afford the enemy no unnecessary advantage in the war in the west. He knew that his every decision must help prop his post's defense and Butler's diplomacy during the long winter ahead.[60]

In the course of the ensuing months, sundry headmen from the western tribes of the Six Nations made their way to Niagara for winter meetings. With the Iroquois beset by agents and propagandists of both

sides, the Confederacy's sachems were finding it difficult to unite their people completely behind their policy of strict neutrality. Most Mohawks remained staunchly loyal to the royalist views of the Johnson family, even though their leaders still conferred peaceably with the rebels whose settlements surrounded their villages. The Oneidas and Tuscaroras proclaimed neutrality but favored the rebel politics of their Presbyterian minister, Samuel Kirkland, while the uncommitted Onondagas wavered from one view to another. The powerful Senecas and Cayugas still waited to determine where their political and commercial interests might best be served. It was with the chiefs of the Senecas, Cayugas, and Onondgas that Butler held "several Conferences" in order "to reclaim their alienated affections."

Caldwell continued to preside over such meetings to lend the required air of ceremony and solemnity, but Butler thereafter became the crown's principal spokesman to the Six Nations. He used a wide range of telling arguments, including those introduced earlier by the colonel, to persuade the Iroquois that their league's neutrality actually benefited the re-

An Iroquois drum. From Lewis Henry Morgan, *League of the Ho-de'-no-sau-nee,* 1851.

An Iroquois war club. From Lewis Henry Morgan, *League of the Ho-de'-no-sau-nee,* 1851.

bels and to remind them of the many benefits they had derived from their ancient alliance with the British king. He also initiated the distruptive but workable practice of promoting the personal interests of the individual sachems and warriors "most ready to attach themselves to Government." Besides appealing to the honor and self-interest of the League and its headmen, Butler also opened Caldwell's storerooms to cater to the Iroquois' weakness for white men's goods. He distributed presents liberally and tapped the kegs to loose a flood of rum that flowed unabated at Niagara throughout the war. While necessary under the adverse circumstances of the moment, such generousity might easily have proved disastrous, for the colonel lacked means to replenish his fort's ever diminishing larder.[61]

A Hungry Winter and an Angry Spring

Even though the rebel invaders of Canada had cut Niagara's principal supply line, Colonel Caldwell and John Butler continued to entertain lavishly every Indian who visited their post throughout the early months of 1776. This hospitality allowed Butler to converse personally with a number of Iroquois, including one party of a hundred Senecas in January or February, much to the displeasure of some of that nation's neutralist headmen. He and Caldwell also handed out written testimonials of loyalty to a number of influential Senecas, including the redoubtable brothers Rowland and John Montour, and by dint of money and liquor Butler kept two old Seneca headmen— one certainly Caldwell's friend Sciawa and the other probably Saweetoa (a war chief also from Genesee Castle)— and a few other Iroquois at his side through the winter and spring. Indian travelers and Butler's couriers spread the agent's speeches throughout the Confederacy. His cajolery and the efforts of the emissaries sent to the Senecas' villages, particularly Lieutenants John and William Johnston, eventually began to have an effect. Missionary Samuel Kirland, by then an official agent of Congress, reported in mid-March "that the face of things among the western tribes of the confederacy begins to change." "It is very evident," he concluded, "their minds are poisoned by some enemy to the liberties of the colonies."[62]

Securing the support or at least the continued neutrality of the Six Nations, while providing no overt aid to the royal cause, nevertheless remained a vital part of Niagara's defense. Early in the year, General Philip Schuyler, the rebels' northern theater commander, seriously con-

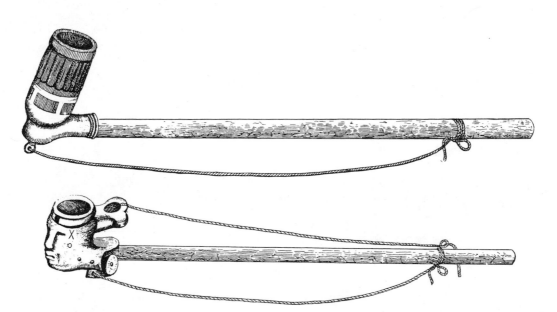

Smoking of pipes was an important part of any formal council. Some Iroquois examples from Lewis Henry Morgan, *League of the Ho-de'-no-sau-nee*, 1851.

templated sending an expedition against the post, but he dared not risk violating the Six Nations' neutrality by marching an army through their lands without first obtaining the sachems' permission, which he knew they would not give. Butler braced up this shield by repeatedly warning the Iroquois that new Englanders from the eastward and Virginians from the southward intended to advance against Niagara, reduce the fort, seize his own person, and then, having eliminated the king's soldiers, "immediately fall upon the six nations & extirpate them from the Earth." Caldwell also contributed by completing all rehabilitation work feasible on Niagara's palisades, and the intelligence that reached Schuyler reported the fort to be "exceedingly well fortified" and "well repaired."

While Niagara's diverse defenses grew stronger, however, its defenders were growing weaker. Caldwell's cupboard began to run bare in February, and he had to put his troops on short rations, supplemented only by what they could commandeer from the traders, hunt in the woods, fish from the icy lake, or barter from the Indians. Despite every effort, by midspring the garrison was reportedly "in a starving condition," the soldiers so demoralized that they seemed ready to surrender without a fight should a rebel force appear at the gate armed with food. In fact, Schuyler entertained the hope that, if many Indians attended some major council held by Butler, they would consume so many of Caldwell's provisions that the British would have to abandon Niagara voluntarily.[63]

Despite their hunger, Caldwell and his King's regulars hung on, and famine conditions did not deter Butler from presenting a bold facade of prosperity and issuing a general invitation for the entire Six Nations to

Gen. Philip Schuyler commanded the Continental Army's northern theater of operations. *Courtesy, William L. Clements Library.*

meet him in council at Niagara in May. Enough trade goods still remained on merchants' shelves to assemble the many presents required for such a conference. He also wrote twice to Guy Johnson's deputy at Pittsburgh, Alexander McKee, ordering him in his own and Caldwell's names to come to Niagara in time to attend this council and to discuss matters he dared not commit to paper "on account of the precariousness of the time." McKee never made the journey because Butler's letters miscarried, but their Iroquois couriers did spread Butler's invitation to all the Senecas and other Indians between Niagara and the forks of the Ohio. As the tribesmen prepared to depart their villages during April, another message from Niagara reached them, this one from Caldwell asking "the Indians not to assemble until he should hear from Detroit."[64]

In the end, Detroit and the spring thaw rescued Caldwell's garrison and Butler's Indian policy. Fort Detroit, unlike Niagara, watched over an extensive *Canadien* agricultural community, which raised enough crops

A watercolor view of Fort Niagara painted about 1784.

and livestock to supplement the dried and salted rations the garrison received from Britain. Caldwell had informed Lieutenant Governor Hamilton of Niagara's predicament, and, as soon as Lake Erie's breaking ice cover permitted, Hamilton dispatched a vessel heavily laded with foodstuff as well as an additional £ 425-worth of Indian goods. Reaching Niagara on May 7, this cargo— and the subsequent ones sent as the schooners *Gage* and *Dunmore* shuttled across Lake Erie—alleviated Caldwell's concerns about food for the immediate future and permitted him to think about taking some action himself to aid the inhabitants of rebel-occupied Canada.

The opening of the lakes traffic allowed the colonel to use the crown's five ships to shift his meager military resources to enhance the prospects of defending the upper posts and the possibilities of acting on the offensive elsewhere. Along with the provisions, he ordered a small detachment of the King's troops (probably 10-20 men) from Detroit to reinforce Niagara immediately, and he also directed Captain De Peyster to send 15-20 additional redcoats from Michilimackinac (the post least exposed to enemy threat) to Detroit and thence to Niagara, where they probably arrived early in June. These transfers added the equivalent of a fifth company for Caldwell to deploy at Niagara or somewhere else. Detroit could spare the men because the two companies of the 18th Regiment that had held Fort Gage at Kaskaskia arrived there on June 3. In response to the need to consolidate his forces when

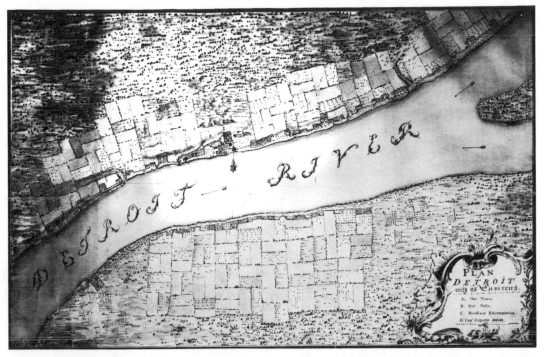

By 1776 the predominently *Canadien* settlement of Detroit was still much as mapped by Lt. John Montresor in 1763. The farms which made Detroit an oasis of agriculture in the Great Lakes wilderness are visible on each side of the fortified village and on the opposite riverbank. *Courtesy, William L. Clements Library.*

the rebels invaded Canada and to orders received from Gage regarding a harebrained western scheme advocated by Virginia's royal governor, Carleton late in 1775 had sent orders for the withdrawal of Kaskaskia's garrison. Captain Hugh Lord's coming added 70 redcoats to Detroit's garrison and made Lord (whose captaincy predated Lernoult's) that post's military commander. The troop movements between Detroit and Niagara were accompanied by an increasing cooperation in the Indian diplomacy conducted at the two posts. Butler used the waterborne postal service to correspond frequently with Jehu Hay, Johnson's resident agent at Detroit, and Hamilton and Hay sometimes shipped Indian delegations across the lake to confer with Butler and Caldwell.[65]

Despite every entreaty by Niagara's statesmen, the Six Nations did not respond to the invitation for a general council there in May. Instead, the colonel and the agent met at various times throughout May and June with envoys from the Six Nations central council, small groups of Indian visitors, and finally the headmen of the Senecas. The first to arrive were emissaries sent by the sachems to inform Caldwell and Butler of the results of a League council held at Onondaga from March 28 to April 2. During the sachems' thorough deliberations over all the messages they had received from both British and Americans (including news of the British evacuation of Boston on March 17), they had often disagreed seriously, with Senecas speaking for those who questioned the advantage of maintaining friendly relations with the rebels. At length, however, the League's wise old men agreed—albeit some of them grudgingly—to maintain the Six Nation's neutrality. They appointed deputies to visit both

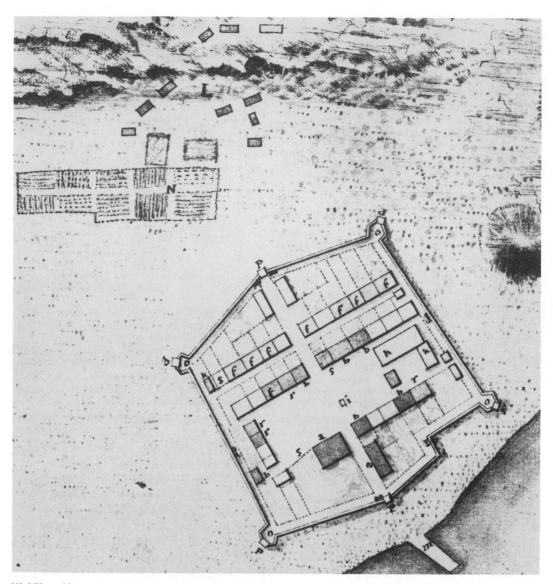

Michilimackinac, surveyed in 1766 by Lt. Perkins Magra. Like Detroit, it was more a stockaded village than a proper fortification. By 1776 the only major addition had been a barracks for the soldiers. Detail from Magra's plan. *Courtesy, William L. Clements Library.*

Albany and Niagara to apprise the representatives of the Congress and the crown alike of the League's official position. These envoys arrived at Niagara at almost the same time as the first ship from Detroit, which delivered a few Ottawas and Chippewas from that post along with its cargo of food. Concurrently, a traveler arrived from the eastward on foot or in canoe bearing a proposal for military action on the part of the troops under Caldwell's command.[66]

This newcomer was James Stanley Goddard, a respected Montreal merchant and veteran of trade and exploration west of Lake Michigan. He had come from Oswegatchie after making a hazardous overland journey from Montreal. Although Governor Carleton had left no instructions for military action in the west when he

50

Capt. George Forster's post at Oswegatchie was a weak wooden fort and the one nearest rebel-occupied Montreal. Detail from "A View of Fort la Galet" drawn by Lt. Thomas Davies in 1760. *Courtesy, National Gallery of Canada.*

fled to Quebec City, Montreal's inhabitants had grown restless under the rebels' military rule, and many prominent British and *Canadien* citizens seem to have plotted amongst themselves to free their city. In particular, rebel plans to curtail the fur trade traffic in the spring prompted the city's merchants to attempt to rally their friends, partners, and customers in *le pays d'en haut* for an effort to drive the enemy from the trade's great entrepôt.

Goddard left the city early in March with only two companions, Claude-Nicholas-Guillaume de Lorimier (the scion of a *Canadien* family long involved in the Indian trade) and Richard Walker (a young Montreal lawyer). Their initial objective was to raise the Indians along the upper St. Lawrence to burn the rebel shipping frozen in Lake Champlain's ice at Ti-conderoga. They reached Oswegatchie about March 9 and convinced Captain Forster of their loyalty and the practicality of striking the rebels in Canada. They adjusted their schemes to whatever ideas Forster entertained, and they persuaded him that the *Canadiens* were ready to join the king's standard should the men of the 8th Regiment carry it to Montreal. Forster could not act, however, before the ice left the St. Lawerence and before he received his colonel's authorization. Hence, while Lorimier set forth in mid-March to recruit Mississauga warriors around the northeastern shores of Lake Ontario, Goddard set off on an arduous trek to Niagara to secure Caldwell's permission and aid for Forster's proposed enterprise.[67]

Everyone along the lower St. Lawrence from the humblest *habitant* to

A pair of light infantrymen sketched in Canada by Lt. John André about 1775. Although these men were probably from the 7th Regiment of Foot, their short coats with shoulder wings and distinctive caps were similar to those worn by Forster's light company of the King's Regiment. *Courtesy, William L. Clements Library.*

across Lake Huron and down the Ottawa River toward Montreal. Goddard then set out directly overland toward Michilimackinac carrying Caldwell's orders and also wampum messages "from the Six Nations inviting the Michilimackinack Indians to assemble at Connesedaga [Canasadaga] village" at the Lake of the Two Mountains west of Montreal. Caldwell directed De Peyster to have the Indians consult with the missionary priests at Canasadaga and then rendezvous with the nearest British regular officer or with John Butler, who apparently hoped to lead an Iroquois force to Canada himself.[69]

Butler, however, found his attempts at recruiting Iroquois warriors stymied by the deputies from Onondaga. He and Caldwell convened a council with these envoys, a number of Senecas, Cayugas, and other Iroquois then about Niagara, and the Chippewas and Ottawas from Detroit. The envoys' report that the Six Nations had confirmed their neutrality displeased the two crown officials, for now that they had a specific military objective in mind Butler hoped to persuade the Iroquois to commit themselves to the British cause. He employed every practiced argument at his command to alter the envoys' resolve, particularly contrasting Britain's military and commercial might with the rebels' weakness and poverty.

Caldwell also spoke out, explaining ingeniously that British forces had evacuated Boston only after tricking the rebels into concentrating all their troops and cannon there, which would allow the Royal Navy to reduce their seaports without opposition. Displaying his growing mastery of Indian diplomacy, he indicated also that, while the navy cut off the rebels' access to European goods, he intended to keep Niagara's trade emporium in British hands. "I shall not give up this post to

the highest-ranking rebel officer expected Caldwell to come to Carleton's assistance, and wild rumors raced down the valley as early as late April that he was bringing the entire King's Regiment and hordes of western Indians against Montreal.[68] In reality, Caldwell's ability to mount any military undertaking remained very limited. He and Butler discussed with Goddard the joint operation the merchant and Forster wished to launch against the rebels around Montreal, and they did agree to furnish Forster what few reinforcements they could muster. Probably at Goddard's request, Caldwell also prepared written orders authorizing Captain De Peyster to assist Goddard's recruiting among the far western tribes and to dispatch any Indian volunteers the Bostonians, without a struggle," he declared; "My men must first fall before the Bostonians shall take possession." The Six Nations deputies, attempting to appease the colonel and the agent, promised to "support the Kings Peace or Government," but this did not include aiding the king's troops against the colonists.

When Butler made his bid to raise warriors to reinforce Forster, the civil chiefs present declined his every importunity. He attempted to induce them to let some warriors sail to Oswegatchie on the pretext of their seeking an early inteview with Guy Johnson, should he return from London, but the headmen recognized his ruse. Ultimately, Butler succeeded in assembling a small group of recruits only by appealing directly to a few adventure-seeking war captains, particularly the Seneca Kanughsgawiat and the Onondaga Kaquatanawji. Under their command, about fifty warrior (mostly Senecas, with a few of the Ottawas and Chippewas, and evidently several Cayugas, Onondagas, and Mohawks) embarked on one of the king's ships about May 10 for the voyage to Forster's post on the St. Lawrence. Butler sent along several of his department's officers, including one or both of the Johnston brothers, and it seems likely that Caldwell's troop transfers allowed him to dispatch a squad or two of redcoats to watch over Forster's fort while the captain led his garrison out to fight.[70]

Niagara's Indian marines disembarked at Oswegatchie on May 12, just in time to join the motley band Forster led forth that day "to deliver the citizens of Montreal from the tyrannical oppression of the rebels." His command totaled 210 men, comprising the 8th's light infantry company (himself, Lieutenants Andrew Parke and Henry Bird, and 38 soldiers), 11 *Canadien* and British traders, and about 160 Mississauga and Iroquois warriors. Later joined by some 60 more *Canadiens* and 44 St. Regis Iroquois, Forster boated down the St. Lawrence to the Cedars (at a rapids 43 miles above Montreal), where on May 19 and 20 he gained impressive triumphs over two rebel detachments. With minimal bloodshed, his men captured an enemy fort, defeated a rebel relief column in the woods and took 500 Continental troops prisoner.

Flush with victory and swollen to nearly 500 with additional Indian and *Canadien* volunteers, Forster's army crossed onto Montreal Island on the 23rd and advanced to within three miles of Lachine before being halted abruptly by reports of a vastly superior rebel force marching to oppose it. Rather than risk a disheartening defeat, Forster retraced his route to the mainland, arranged a prisoner exchange with the rebels, and late on the 30th retired toward Oswegatchie. Although Forster failed to oust the rebels from Montreal, his remarkable achievements (which later won him a promotion to major of the 21st Regiment of Foot) caused chaos among the rebel troops at Montreal at the very moment rebel generals were vainly trying to assemble sufficient force to stop a more dangerous advance from Quebec City. The first units of a large relief expedition from Britain had landed at Quebec on May 6, chased off the rebels still besieging that city, and provided Carleton with the troops he needed for a methodical but uninspired campaign that drove the last Continental soldier back into New York on June 18, 1776.[71]

On the Sidelines of the Revolution

While Captain Forster's light infantry company was striking the 8th Regiment's first wartime blow at the Cedars, Colonel Caldwell and John Butler remained at Niagara trying to assemble more Indian warriors. Butler seemed optimistic, and in mid-May, 1776, he sent a letter to inform Sir John Johnson that he had gathered "a considerable body of Indians ready to go on service." He only waited, he wrote, to receive news of Guy Johnson's return "or orders to proceed." He evidently hoped to cooperate with Sir John in some long-anticipated effort to re-establish royal authority in the Mohawk Valley as well as along the St. Lawrence. For nearly a year, from his headquarters at Johnson Hall, Sir John had been covertly organizing a loyalist regiment among his friends, neighbors, and tenants, rallying Iroquois sympathizers, and exchanging itelligence with British officials at New York City, Montreal, and Niagara.

Championing the crown's cause in the midst of many Congress supporters, however, was a risky business. In January General Philip Schuyler had marched a large militia force to Johnstown, compelled Sir John to accept a parole promising peaceful behavior, and disarmed many of his followers. Not deterred by the loss of weapons or by a parole he considered illegal, Sir John had vigorously renewed his intrigues. He corresponded frequently with Caldwell and Butler by means of Mohawk couriers, and the colonel reportedly employed Seneca packmen to carry a new stockpile of guns and ammunition to Johnson Hall. When Butler's letter reached the Hall on May 22, however, its intended recipient had been gone for three days.

Johnson had found it impossible to conceal his activities from his many enemies, and in mid-May Schuyler sent Colonel Elias Dayton with his 3rd New Jersey Regiment to arrest him and his adherents. Forewarned of his danger, Sir John abandoned his home and pregnant wife on May 19. Gathering a band of 170 loyal Scottish tenants, 100 members of their families, and 3 Mohawks as guides, he fled northward into the wilderness the following day. Before leaving Johnson Hall, he dispatched John Deserontyon, a Mohawk war captain, to Niagara with news of his plight and also with letters for Caldwell from General Howe at Boston (dated January 11) and New York royal governor William Tryon warning of rebel intentions to attack Niagara.

As soon as Deserontyon arrived at Niagara, Caldwell dispatched a vessel to Oswegatchie with twenty-five barrels of pork, twenty-five more of flour, plus some rum and sugar to feed Johnson's party. Johnson's band actually emerged from the woods farther down the St. Lawrence at St. Regis about June 5 after a terrible sixteen-day march during which their provisions had run out and they had gone "nine days without any thing to subsist upon but wild onion root & the leaves of the Beach Trees." With Caldwell's food and some artillery forwarded by Forster, Johnson descended the river to Montreal, where he arrived on the 17th, only a few hours after British troops had reoccupied the city. Thereafter, he remained in Montreal, where he headquartered the loyalist regiment he was then able to raise openly.[72]

Johnson Hall, erected by Sir William in 1763. Following his death it was occupied by his son, John. *Courtesy, New York State Office of Parks, Recreation and Historic Preservation, Johnson Hall State Historic Site Saratoga/Capital Region.*

Deserontyon's report of Sir John's flight meant that Caldwell would not have to support or supervise a Mohawk Valley campaign immediately, a fortuitous circumstance because Butler was discovering that he could not manipulate the Six Nations as easily as he had supposed. Several large parties of both Lower and Upper Senecas journeyed to Niagara late in May in response to Butler's earlier invitation. The delegations were led by the tribe's most important headmen: Sayenqueraghta and Adongot (principal civil and war chiefs respectively from the Genesee region), and Kayashuta and Cauchcauchcauteda (Flying Crow) (foremost civil and war chiefs of the Allegheny villages). Also present were the old Genesee chiefs Sciawa and Saweetoa, probably some other Iroquois, a few Shawnees and Munsees from the Ohio country, and several representatives of the tribes about Detroit.

Kayashuta's party arrived by way of Fort Erie (then held by Lieutenant John Burnett and some forty red-

coats) and Fort Schlosser in company with a white man from Pittsburgh, Paul Long. Long's presence aroused Caldwell's suspicions. Ever alert for enemy plots against his post, he had Butler question Long about his loyalties and about affairs at Fort Pitt, and he then had four of his own officers interrogate the man for two days. Finally, he had Long brought to his own office, where, Long reported, he "attempted to frighten me to a confession." Long, in reality a spy for the rebels' Pittsburgh Indian agent, impressed them all with his seemingly consistent story and his apparent honesty, and Caldwell permitted him to witness the council that followed.

In the fort's chapel from May 31 through June 7 the colonel presided daily over Butler's meetings with the Seneca headmen.[73] After preaching friendship, loyalty, and neutrality to the Indians for the past year, the British spokesmen now plainly appealed to the Iroquois to take up their hatchets for King George, a proposal that so disturbed and divided the headmen

Elias Dayton, colonel of the 3rd New Jersey Regiment, arrived too late to apprehend Sir John Johnson. *Courtesy, William L. Clements Library.*

that they debated among themselves for two days before delivering their reply. Fully expecting a favorable response, Caldwell and Butler were shocked by the speech Kayashuta delivered on behalf of his nation. Charging that the British sought to involve the Indians in an unnecessary war, he told Butler "that you are the mad, foolish, crazy & deceitful person —— for you think we are fools & advise us to do what is not our interest."

Thoroughly disconcerted, the two crown officials adjourned the meeting for the day while they regrouped. Their arguements were somewhat redeemed by the propitious return of a number of warriors with three scalps and a prisoner they had taken with Forster's army at the Cedars. Hanging up the scalps—the first of many to come to Niagara during the Revolution—in the chapel, Caldwell and Butler remarked that "the Fiddler was now getting in Tune for the Americans to dance by." When the council resumed, Butler cannily let one of his Mohawk friends extoll the wisdom of assisting the militarily superior vic-

tors of the Cedars fight, while the agent himself pointed out that the British would always be able to supply the Iroquois with abundant and low-priced trade goods.

Nevertheless, every argument failed to sway the senior Seneca chiefs, and Cauchcauchcauteda and others bluntly refuted Butler's logic. Only three headmen—the old chiefs Sciawa and Saweetoa and the Genesee war captain Adongot—agreed that the Six Nations ought to support the crown actively, and they helped influence about fifty additional warriors (mostly Senecas) to join a few more Detroit Indians in boarding a vessel bound for the St. Lawrence. Even so, Butler had to back off from his attempt to muster a major Six Nations levy because, Long reported, "the majority declared against it or having any thing to do with the dispute." Upon leaving Niagara, most of the Seneca leaders repaired to a League council meeting at Onondaga in mid-June, where they attempted to mend their confederacy's fraying neutrality and denounced Butler's meddling in their affairs.[74]

Despite this setback, the coming of summer in 1776 brought a succession of generally good news to crown officials at Niagara. The British recapture of Canada eased Caldwell's dilemma with provisions and other supplies and also reduced somewhat his scarcity of manpower. Throughout the shipping season, convoys of bateaux ferried merchandise from the docks at Quebec and Montreal to Oswegatchie, whence the lakes shipping delivered it to the anxiously waiting troops and traders at Niagara, Detroit, and Michiliamackinac. Because of the heavy demands placed upon the provincial navy, Caldwell, approving an arrangement made at Detroit by Commodore Grant, ordered the sailors' daily fare augmented by an extra half-ration as of July 24. Niagara's private commerce also began to revive, and that summer the firm of (William) Taylor & (William) Duffin, Edward Pollard's principal competitor, constructed two sizable stables and an even larger tavern, no doubt to serve the many newcomers reaching the post. Among them came additional British regulars for the colonel.[75]

Early in August, Captain Andrew Parke (promoted for his part in the Cedars campaign) delivered to Niagara a party of redcoated recruits recently arrived in Canada from England, and a month later Caldwell was also able to incorporate Captain Hugh Lord's two companies of the Royal Irish into his own regiment. Because of the diminished and scattered state of the 18th Regiment in America, the ministry had previously determined that its officers and non-commissioned officers should be returned to England to rebuild it from scratch. When Carleton's directive to this effect reached the interior, Caldwell drafted the 18th's western veterans into the 8th's companies at Detroit and Niagara and ordered Lord and his officers home, thereby returning command of the Detroit garrison to the trusty Captain Lernoult. The recruits, raw and seasoned, augmented Niagara's garrison by perhaps another fifty regulars.[76]

The infusion of men and materiel, which was not completed until autumn, not only improved that state of Caldwell's defenses but also significantly enhanced Butler's leverage with the Six Nations. The restocking of the king's and merchants' storehouses at Niagara allowed the agent to make good his oft-repeated assertion that only the British could furnish the Iroquois with the many European manufactures necessary for their well-being. Adding further weight to Butler's commercial rea-

Sir John Johnson. Portait by John Mare, 1772. *Courtesy, New York State Office of Parks, Recreation and Historic Preservation, Johnson Hall State Historic Site, Saratoga/Capital Region.*

soning was the rebels' simultaneous embargo of their own trade with the Iroquois. Despite the war, Albany and Schenectady merchants dispatched their usual spring consignments westward that year, sending bateaux up the Mohawk River bound for the Fort Stanwix-Oneida Lake portage and thence Oswego and the upper posts. This traffic alarmed rebel authorities, who feared that the cargoes would be commandeered by Caldwell to supply his garrisons or to outfit a Johnson-led invasion force.

Initially, General Schuyler directed Mohawk Valley authorities to permit no bateaux to pass beyond Fort Stanwix except those destined to trade at designated villages in Six Nations country. Upon learning in late May that a few Iroquois had gone to Canada to fight for the British, however, he ordered the militia to stop "all such batteaux as were designed for the upper country." By thus cutting off the remaining trade from the east,

An Iroquois war club. From Lewis Henry Morgan, *League of the Ho-de'-no-sau-nee*, 1851.

the rebels shortsightedly deprived the westernmost of the Six Nations of any ready, reliable source of merchandise other than traders based at Niagara. Of equal consequence, Schuyler also determined early in June to garrison and refortify Fort Stanwix, which Colonel Dayton's regiment actually did in mid-July with-

The hired sailors of the Naval Department kept provisions and supplies moving to the British posts on the Great Lakes. *Drawing by Joe Lee.*

out first informing the Six Nations' sachems. Thus, a year after declaring its neutrality, the League of the Iroquois found its territory bracketed by two forts: Stanwix on the east meant to cut off trade and communications, and Niagara to the west maintained as a trade emporium.[77]

The posting of Continental troops at Fort Stanwix posed new problems for Caldwell. With the stoppage of the Albany-Schenectady trade and the flight of Sir John Johnson, he had lost his primary sources of current news about rebel activities in New York. The resultant want of intelligence, coupled with a possible military threat to Niagara or perhaps Oswego from the enemy at Fort Stanwix, necessitated his establishing a more extensive network of Niagara-based scouts and spies, usually loyalists and Indians recruited by Butler. In fact, an increasing number of men journeyed to and from Niagara during the summer of 1776 as the Revolutionary conflict intensified across the northern frontier. And the spies who departed the fort were not all Caldwell's. Paul Long, of course, carried an extensive report about Niagara and its defenders back to Pittsburgh, and on June 27 Peter and Richard Ryckman (Albany traders who had wintered at the fort) slipped away and, in company with 21 Senecas, carried similar information to rebel authorities in the Mohawk Valley. The Senecas seemed resolved, moreover, to make matters difficult for the British. Early in July, following the recent council at Onondaga, Sayenqueraghta returned to Niagara to inform Caldwell of the League's latest profession of its neutrality. When he left again for his village, he took back with him most of the Senecas and other Iroquois who had been hanging about the post at Butler's bidding.[78]

On the other hand, rebel efforts to consolidate their control throughout backcountry New York and Pennsylvania compelled more and more loyalists to seek refuge in Canada or at Niagara. From among the men who reached Niagara, Butler selected those he trusted for positions in his expanding Indian Department. One of these, strangely, was a cousin of Caldwell's. William Caldwell, a thirtyish native of County Fermanagh, had come to America late in 1773 to visit a wealthy uncle in Philadelphia. Shortly afterward, he had made his way to the Pennsylvania frontier, where he had become involved in Governor Dunmore's campaign against the Shawnees and fought in the Battle of Point Pleasant. During the ensuing year-and-a-half he had journeyed to Ireland and back to America, carried dispatches for Dunmore, and joined Pennsylvania forces in 1775 on an expedition against the Connecticut settlements in the Susquehanna's Wyoming Valley.

Once back in Philadelphia, Caldwell eventually ran afoul of his uncle's radical politics and the city's rebel miitia. Abandoning some property and an expected inheritance, he fled north through the colony in June, 1776, followed by rebel bulletins describing him as "a tall young man, [with] fair complexion," wearing a blue coat. Along the trail he joined

A soldier of a battalion company of the 8th Regiment of Foot as he would have appeared in 1774-1785. *Drawing by Joe Lee.*

forces with four captured British officers (taken prisoner when St. Johns capitulated in November, 1775) who were escaping rebel custody. Finding a loyalist guide in William Johnston (probably the same as the lieutenant in Butler's Indian service), they soon reached Niagara. There William Caldwell obtained a lieutenancy in the Indian Department and began a long career as Britain's most active and successful partisan officer on the northern frontier.[79]

A second young officer destined to achieve notoriety in New York's backcountry warfare also arrived at Niagara about that time. He was John Butler's eldest son Walter, a newly-commissioned ensign in the King's Regiment. Walter Butler, then a 23-year-old aspiring lawyer, had gone with his father and the other members of Guy Johnson's entourage from the Mohawk Valley to Oswego and then to Montreal the previous summer. As one of Johnson's hastily-

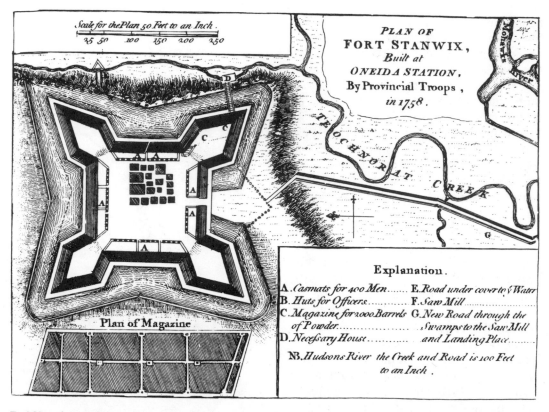

recruited Indian Department officers, he distinguished himself in September, 1775, in skirmishes around the British post at St. Johns and in the repulse of Ethan Allen's attempted *coup-de-main* against Montreal. When the situation deteriorated in October and Johnson decided to flee Canada, John Butler persuaded his son to accompany Johnson's party to England "for his improvement." Debarking from the armed ship *Adamant* at Falmouth in late December, Johnson's company made its way to London, where Walter, bearing Governor Carleton's hearty recommendation to the secretary at war, sought a place in the British army in America.

Referred to Edmund Armstrong, agent for the 8th Regiment, Walter Butler received or purchased an en-signcy postdated to November 22, 1775. Armstrong entrusted the King's new subaltern with letters and financial statements for the regiment's officers at Niagara, and Walter set out for America at once, evidently boarding a vessel in February, most likely one bound for Halifax. His subsequent movements remain a mystery. He may have joined the British expedition that sailed from Halifax to capture New York City and then proceeded across country to Niagara. More likely, he snowshoed immediatey to besieged Quebec or waited until he learned of its relief in May before taking a ship there. In any event, he was at Niagara by early autumn, taking part in Indian councils held by his father. In October, however, Colonel Caldwell would send Ensign Butler to take command of Fort

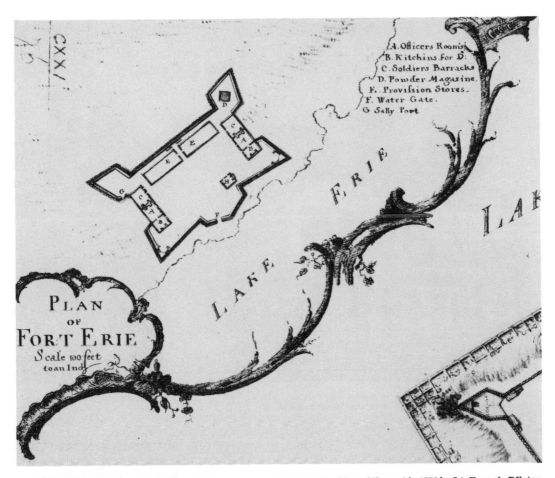

A. Officers Rooms
B. Kitchins for D.
C. Soldiers Barracks
D. Powder Magazine.
E. Provision Stores.
F. Water Gate.
G Sally Port

LAKE ERIE

LAKE

LAK

PLAN
OF
FORT ERIE
Scale 100 feet
to an Inch

Ens. Walter Butler's first duty at Niagara was command of Fort Erie. Plan of the post in 1773 by Lt. Francis Pfister. *Courtesy, British Library, Crown Maps, cxxi, 76.*

Erie, a post he apparently held until he joined his father's yet unofficial corps of rangers the following spring.[80]

No opportunity arose during the summer of 1776 for Colonel Caldwell to call upon the military skills of either Walter Butler or William Caldwell, however, or to try again to recruit Sayenqueraghta's warriors, to a large extent because the reopening of communications subjected him again to the directives of General Carleton. A cautious commander and conventional tactician who hoped to end the rebellion through reconciliation rather than by retaliation, Carleton never issued orders for Caldwell to employ his redcoats or Indian allies against the rebels in any manner.

In fact, he contemplated an operation from Niagara only once—and then only at the insistence of his second-in-command, Major General John Burgoyne, and Sir John Johnson.

Almost as soon as Montreal fell to the British, Burgoyne proposed that Carleton send a detachment of troops and Indians against the Mohawk Valley, a plan that he had first heard from Guy Johnson in London and that he outlined with Sir John Johnson in Montreal. Sir John assured Burgoyne—and both assured Carleton—that such an expedition would encounter little opposition because the Six Nations and white settlers were "strongly attached to His majesty" and would, by threatening Albany, both aid General Howe's campaign

The "large stone house", popularly known today as the "French Castle", accommodated most of Fort Niagara's officers. The officers' mess was also located in the building.

against New York City and disrupt rebel efforts to hold Lake Champlain against Carleton's own advance. Such a maneuver appealed to Carleton at first. "The Rebels are driven from this province," he wrote to Captain Forster at Oswegatchie on June 20, and "I am preparing to follow them, and shall send a force up to Lake Ontario to penetrate that way also into their provinces." He implied that Forster would command this expedition as an adjunct to his own operations on Lake Champlain. He instructed Forster to coordinate matters with Caldwell and to "make all preparations you can, and have ready all the force you can collect, to join what you may require from hence [Montreal]."

What preparations Caldwell and Forster made in response to this dispatch are not known, but Burgoyne envisioned and promoted a more ambitious operation than Carleton was

suggesting. Burgoyne proposed that he personally command a force composed of "three British Battalions, with a corps of artillery, some Canadians & a large body of Indians," plus Sir John's partly-formed regiment. Carleton contemplated this plan favorably for a month, though he seemed disinclined to entrust its execution to Burgoyne. In a letter of July 19 he informed Caldwell that, although he had not yet decided to mount this operation, he now considered it "too considerable for Captain Forster." Instead, he proposed that Caldwell, part of the King's Regiment, and John Butler's departmental officers and Indians might form the core of the expeditionary force.

The governor directed the colonel to submit his opinions about the plan, to foward all available intelligence about rebel strength on the New York frontier, and "to keep the savages ready at a call and well disposed to act." Carleton still expressed some doubts about the practicability of such an expedition, but he promised to give Caldwell "timely notice" should Niagara's garrison be called upon to undertake it. Yet within a week—before the colonel even received the letter—Carleton changed his mind and ordered the plan abandoned. His reason for doing so, he told a disbelieving Burgoyne, was "want of a sufficient store of provision" for the troops and Indians.[81]

By mid-August, therefore, Caldwell learned that neither he nor his King's regulars would be required to participate in what remained of the northern campaign of 1776. Concurrently, he was apprised that he and Butler would not straightway have to attempt again to recruit warrior auxiliaries from among the unwilling Iroquois. Carleton had also written on July 19 to Caldwell—and to each of the other upper post commanders—to report that he was sending home all the Indians who were then coming down from Michilimackinac. Acting on Caldwell's instructions, Captain De Peyster, with the aid of Goddard and other merchants, had mustered some 500 warriors from seven tribes bordering or beyond Lake Michigan and dispatched them down the Ottawa River to help the British drive the rebels from Canada. By the time the first Michilimackinac parties reached Montreal in mid-July, however, the rebels had retreated to Ticonderoga, and Carleton decided he wanted no Indian assistance in pursuing them into New York. Therefore, he had each arriving party greeted with feasts and gifts and then promptly dismissed. Carleton advised his western officials of this action, implying that he wished them to refrain from sending any more Indians down that year. Rather, he desired them to prevail upon the Indians "to hold themselves in readiness to cooperate

A British officer and merchant at Fort Niagara. *Drawing by Joe Lee.*

with His Majesty's Arms next Spring."[82]

With the receipt of Carleton's instructions regarding the Indians and of his cancellation of the proposed expedition, Caldwell's principal responsbility—after the defense of Niagara—became readying his regiment and the nearby Indians to take the field in 1777 should the situation require it. Convincing the main body of Iroquois warriors to enter a war their sachems had wished and still hoped to avoid, however, would require a diplomacy both intensified and well coordinated. Sometime during August, Agent Jehu Hay arrived in person from Detroit to advise Caldwell and Butler about Lieutenant Governor Hamilton's dealings with the midwestern tribes. Shortly after Hay set sail for Montreal to seek an audience with Carleton, the colonel kindled the council fire for the largest and most important gathering of Indians over which he had yet presided.[83]

The Colonel's Last Service

Colonel Caldwell and John Butler resumed their stalled efforts to win over the Six Nations in their long-contemplated general council, which began at Niagara in late August, 1776. This conference attracted spokesmen from each of the six confederated tribes as well as from several of their satellite tribes and the nearby Mississaugas. Only the westernmost of the Six Nations, however, were fairly represented. The Senecas, Cayugas, and Onondagas came in large numbers with several of their important headmen, including Butler's Seneca friends Adongot, Sciawa, and Saweetoa, the Onondaga speaker Teyawarunte, the Cayuga chief Ojageghte (Fish-Carrier), and evidently the great Seneca leader Sayenqueraghta. Conversely, only a few Oneidas, Tuscaroras, and Mohawks attended, none of them noted sachems or chiefs. Nevertheless, the appearance of at least one or two chiefs from each of the six tribes allowed Butler to cloak the decisions and messages em-

A large vessel of the Naval Department at Niagara about 1784. Although shown rigged as a schooner, the artist might actually have intended to depict the snow-rigged *Haldimand* or the *Seneca* built in 1777.

anating from the conference with the legitimacy of Six Nations approbation. Furthermore, several of the chiefs had come directly from a major council at German Flats at which the rebels' Indian commissioners had foolishly affronted the Six Nations with a rudely-delivered ultimatum threatening massive military retaliation should a single Iroquois warrior strike another blow against the colonists. The Niagara meeting therefore convened under promising circumstances for the British, and Caldwell and Butler made the most of them.[84]

Once again Butler forcefully pleaded the necessity for the Six Nations to make a unanimous endorsement of the crown's position. He submitted to them, he recalled in 1785, "that it was not only their duty to the King their Father, but their Interest, to attach themselves to his cause." He warned them not to heed the lying words of the rebels at Albany and Pittsburgh, and he assured them that he now "had arms ammunition & all other necessaries to serve them three years." Caldwell, although not in the best of health, also played his part. He presided over the sessions in Niagara's council house in company with his junior officers. He personally reminded the tribesmen "that he had long advised them to lay hold of the King's hand, that if they did not they would be cut off, but if they did they would live hereafter." Both he and Butler also told the Indians that Governor Carleton wished them well and that his commands would determine their future role in the conflict.

At the end of the first week of September, while the council still met,

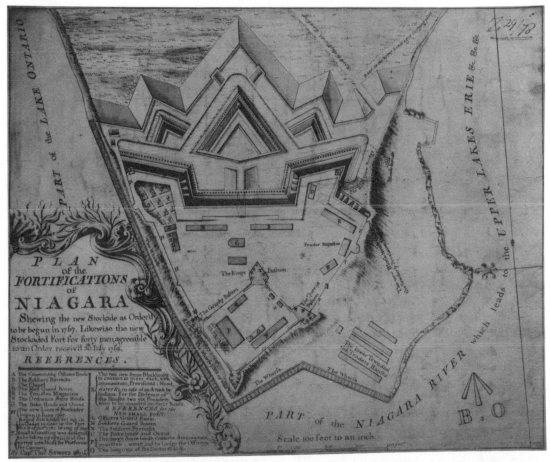

Capt. Thomas Sowers' 1768 plan depicts Niagara much as it was in 1776. The chapel "C" was the site of many of Lt. Col. Caldwell's Indian councils and the probable location of his burial. *Plan in the British War Office, Caxton House, London in 1929 but now believed lost.*

the royal schooner *Gage* anchored off Fort Erie and set ashore a deputation of the leading civil and war chiefs of the Detroit-area Wyandots, Ottawas, Potawatomis, and Chippewas. Lieutenant Governor Hamilton had sent them at Caldwell's suggestion that envoys from these so-called "Lakes Tribes" might have a good effect on the Iroquois gathering at Niagara, and their presence did help pressure the Six Nations chiefs to declare openly for the British before other tribes replaced theirs in the king's favor. Headed by Sastaretsi (also known as Dawatong), the principal civil chief of the Detroit Wyandots, the envoys reported that the Lakes and Ohio tribes had just agreed at a council with Hamilton to support the British and to form an alliance among themselves. Moreover, the deputies explained that the northern and southern tribes, with the blessing of royal officials, were reviving long-frustrated plans for a defensive inter-tribal coalition. This new cooperation among the midwestern tribes and between them and the British threatened to undermine the profitable and prestigious balance-of-power role the Six Nations had long maintained by acting as intermediary between the king's officials and the other northern tribes. This possibility, added to Butler's many political and economic arguments, finally moved many individuals among the League's west-

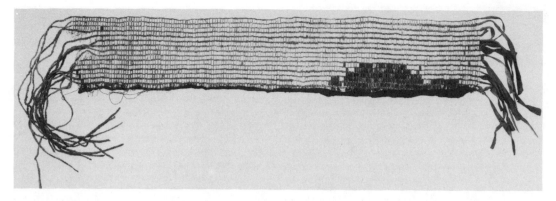

This fragment is believed part of the six foot belt of white wampum with a beaver of purple or black woven into one end which was presented to Sastaretsi's Wyandots by the Seneca at Niagara. The beading was originally about thirty rows wide. *Courtesy, Smithsonian Institution, Department of Anthropology, Catalog #391,891.*

ern nations to abandon or ignore the decisions and promises made by their central council at Onondaga.[85]

When Butler offered the king's hatchet belt to the Indians in attendance many—but not all—of the Iroquois accepted it. Evidently most of the Senecas present declared for the British, as did may of the Cayugas and Onondagas, although these latter were far from unanimous. The few Oneidas, Tuscaroras, and Mohawks then at Niagara also opted for alliance with the British, but they represented neither their tribal leaders nor people. The Iroquois who accepted Butler's wampum, moreover, did not commit themselves to taking up the hatchet against the colonists immediately. Rather, they bound themselves to the nascent pro-British coalition among the midwestern and southern tribes, the first intention of which, Sayenqueraghta reminded the Wyandots in 1779, was "that you was to watch and guard your Country against the Enemy on the Ohio, and we to do the same on our Side." To seal this pact, the Senecas evidently at this time presented to the Wyandots, as head of the Lakes confederacy, a large belt of white wampum, six feet long with a beaver of purple beads woven into one end.

The British, the Lakes Tribes and the Senecas and their Iroquois adherents thereby agreed "mutually to assist each other as far as lay in our Power." As had happened at Detroit, some of the king's newly-professed allies also expressed an eagerness "to rise and fall upon the frontiers" at once. But Caldwell, as had Hamilton, disappointed these warriors by refusing his consent. Though he and Butler were simply obeying Carleton's strictures, they told the Iroquois that they advocated patience because premature hostilities would endanger the Mohawks, whose villages lay open to swift retaliation by the rebels. The two officials made it clear that until Carleton gave his authorization the Indians must hold any war plans in abeyance.[86]

The outcome of this council marked a turning point in Britain's wartime relations with the Six Nations and a major success for the diplomacy of Butler and Caldwell. Even though only a portion of the Confederacy had succumbed to their persuasions, Butler reported happily: "at my Instance they sent proper Messages to their Westen Brethren to prevail upon them to follow their Example." The wampum that went back to Detroit and also to Michilimackinac for dissemination to the League's old allies among the Lakes, Ohio, Wabash, and far western tribes announced that the Six Nations had joined the intertribal coalition previously formed by the midwestern nations. As the council drew to a close on September 18, the assembled chiefs also had Butler commit to paper a speech that they wished to accompany a large wampum belt they were sending to the Oneidas, Tuscaroras and Mohawks urging them "to quit the Bostonians." Their speech related their determination to stand by the king and implored those three tribes to do likewise. After the conference ended, many of the Iroquois remained to sample Niagara's hospitality well into October.[87]

Caldwell and Butler believed they had succeeded in readying a sizable part of the Six Nations to serve with the British whenever Carleton so ordered and that without their accords with the Iroquois, as Butler stated, "the upper Posts could not have been preserved or at least protected from the Insults of the Enemy." Butler invited the departing Indians to return to Niagara, but not until they had completed their seasonal hunting. He was not yet ready to proceed against Albany and would remain at the fort for the winter, he explained to them, because the year had advanced too far to begin a campaign. In reality, he had not received any further instructions from Carleton. Many of the Indians, however, suspected that the British had postponed operations because Colonel Caldwell had fallen too dangerously ill to lead his troops.[88]

In one of his reports early in October, Caldwell himself had confessed to Carleton that his "ill state of health" hindered his discharging his duties. Before this worrisome news reached the governor, however, Carleton had commanded his much-delayed operations on Lake Champlain. Prior to setting his fleet and army in motion, he had determined that he

Wyandot chief Sastaretsi headed a delegation of "Lakes Tribes" which met with Lt. Col. Caldwell in September 1776. Sketch by Lt. Gov. Henry Hamilton. *By permission of the Houghton Library, Harvard University.*

would not be able to dislodge the rebels from their stronghold at Ticonderoga and that he could aspire to do no more before winter set in than destroy their fleet on the lake. He therefore assumed that, unless Howe's campaign against New York City succeeded in ending the Revolution, it would require a final campaign in 1777 to subdue the enemy. In consequence, on October 6 he instructed his senior officials at Niagara, Detroit, and Michilimackinac to prepare the Indians of their districts for participation in the coming year's war effort as auxiliaries to a British army.

Carleton explained his current operations and intentions in identical language to each official, though his orders regarding the Indians differed slightly in each instance in accord-

Gilded officers' buttons, 8th Regiment of Foot. Both styles have been excavated at sites in the Great Lakes region. *Drawings by Marbud Prozeller.*

ance with the role the various tribes might best play in a strategy directed specifically against the rebel armies in New York. Since Niagara's proximity to the front allowed it to take an active part in the war, he wrote Caldwell that "I should be glad you have directions that all which can be spared of the 8th Regiment & all Indians of your neighbourhood be prepared to take the field early in the spring." By the time these instructions—and several later missives regarding the lakes shipping and other matters—were delivered at Niagara, however, it was no longer in Caldwell's power to serve his king further.[89]

The King's colonel had succumbed to his lengthy, unidentified illness on October 31. He may have suffered from chronic poor health, for he is known to have visited the mineral springs at Bath at least twice (in 1770 and 1773), but Niagara's harsh, sometimes hungry winters tested the hardiest constitutions. For a man who had once considered himeself "a stranger in this Indian world," however, Caldwell had adapted relatively well. He had been honored with an Iroquois name, "Oquhaenjes" (or "Oghweanjeyo"), and as he lay dying, his nephew John informed the family, two Six Nations chiefs (most likely the old Senecas Sciawa and Saweetoa) went to his door to bid their dear friend farewell. "Let us," they asked with tears streaming from their eyes, "let us, but touch him be-

fore he dies, and we will be contented." It may be assumed that many Iroquois and Mississaugas, as well as John Butler and William Caldwell, joined the men of the King's Regiment in conducting a military funeral for their respected lieutenant colonel, probably on the first of November.[90]

Caldwell's passing left a serious void in British command structure in the west. When Carleton eventually learned of this loss late in January, 1777, he immediately appointed Major Mason Bolton of the 9th Regiment of Foot to fill the vacant lieutenant colonelcy in the 8th. By then, of course, the weather prevented Bolton from traveling to his new post. Fortunately, Detroit heard of the tragedy before Lake Erie froze over. As senior officer then in the region, Captain Lernoult hurried to Niagara during the second week of November to assume the command of the regiment, posts, and many problems that Caldwell had managed since 1774.[91]

John Caldwell, lieutenant colonel of the 8th (King's) Regiment of Foot, had commanded at Niagara for twenty-seven months during which he had not once unsheathed his own sword against any of his king's enemies. With little evidence about Caldwell's abilities as a military leader to report, the surviving records of his tenure neither reveal very much about his qualities as an administrator or his attitudes toward the American revolutionaries. Nonetheless, they do indicate that Caldwell performed competently the wide variety of duties that became the standard business of every British officer who commanded a post along the Revolutionary frontier. Foremost in all matters, he adhered conscientiously to the orders he received from his commander-in-chief, whether Haldimand, Gage, or Carleton. Because of the incertitudes of communications to and from the frontier posts, however, these orders were often outdated when they reached him or deliberately indefinite or simply lacking altogether, as during the bleak winter of 1775-1776. Time and again, therefore, Caldwell had no choice but to rely upon his own best judgment in situations with which he had little practical experience. The mark of a good commander—one infrequently exhibited by British officers of the period—was the mettle to make decisions and take initiatives without always waiting approval from higher authority. That Caldwell possessed this quality was revealed when he committed what limited forces he could muster to assail the rebels in Canada in the spring of 1776.

In most cases, however, Caldwell's reponsibilities had concerned matters more closely related to his own post. The defense of Niagara's fort and portage always claimed his first priority, moreso after the disgraceful capture of Ticonderoga by the rebels. Proper defense demanded that he attend to several related tasks: the adequate repair and never-ending maintenance of the forts' physical works; the timely acquisition and conservation of all supplies, especially foodstuffs; the most advantageous deployment and employment of always scarce manpower; the prudent management of the indispensable sailing vessels; and the continual collection and evaluation of frontier intelligence. Furthermore, the defense of Niagara and its trade compelled him to master Indian diplomacy himself and also to rely implicitly upon the Indian Department officials assigned to his post. Especially after

Fort Niagara's chapel stood on the site of the modern flagpoles. At least three British officers are known to have been buried beneath the building between 1759 and 1795. The chapel probably served as Lt. Col. Caldwell's final resting place as well.

the outbreak of colonial rebellion, the amity and alliance of the Six Nations became an integral part of Caldwell's defenses by providing a buffer between Niagara and its enemies to the east and south.

Caldwell's success as a wilderness statesman, first as the crown's sole spokesman and later as Butler's *ex officio* assistant, was attested by the results of his last council and by the friendships he established with several of the Iroquois. Caldwell typified Britain's post commanders in all these matters, but in particular in the proficiency with which he performed unfamiliar duties in strange surroundings. If he had come to the mouth of the Niagara River as a stranger, he remains so no longer. In a yet unlocated and unmarked grave probably beneath the fort's chapel, he rests still by Lake Ontario's cold shore.

LIST OF ABBREVIATIONS

(Complete information is given in the Select Bibliography.)

Am. Arch.	Peter Force, comp., *American Archives...*
B&ECHS	Buffalo & Erie County Historical Society, Buffalo, N.Y.
BHC	Burton Historical Collection, DPL
BHCL	*Burton Historical Collection Leaflet*
BL Add. MSS.	British Library Additional Manuscripts
CHR	*Canadian Historical Review*
CLP	Carnegie Library of Pittsburgh, Pa.
CO	Colonial Office Papers, series/volume, PRO
DAR	Kenneth G. Davies, ed., *Documents of the American Revolution*
DCB	*Dictionary of Canadian Biography*
DPL	Detroit Public Library, Detroit, Mich.
Draper MSS.	Lyman C. Draper Manuscripts, State Historical Society of Wisconsin, Madison, Wisc.
DRCHC	Adam Shortt and Arthur G. Doughty, eds., *Documents Relating to the Constitutional History of Canada*
Gage Corr.	Thomas Gage, *The Correspondence of...*
GMLB I-III	George Morgan Letterbooks I-III, 1775-1779, CLP
GMLB 1776	George Morgan Letterbook for 1776, PHMC
HMC	Great Britain, Historical Manuscripts Commission
HP/	Sir Frederick Haldimand Papers, British Library, London/appropriate manuscript or published source (original manuscripts are cited as BM Add. MSS.)
JP	William Johnson, *The Papers of Sir William Johnson*
JRUL	John Rylands University Library of Manchester, England
MG	Manuscript Group
MPHSC	Michigan State Pioneer and Historical Society, *Collections*
MVHR	*Mississippi Valley Historical Review*
NYCD	Edmund B. O'Callaghan and Berthold Fernow, eds., *Documents Relative to the Colonial History of the State of New-York*
NYH	*New York History*
NYPL	New York Public Library, New York City, N.Y.
OH	*Ontario History*
PAC	Public Archives of Canada, Ottawa, Ont.
PCC	Papers of the Continental Congress, 1774-1789, National Archives and Records Service, Washington, D.C.
PHMC	Pennsylvania Historical and Museum Commission, Harrisburg, Pa.
Phyn & Ellice LB	Letterbooks of Phyn and Ellice, 1767-1776, B&ECHS
PMHB	*Pennsylvania Magazine of History and Biography*
PRO	Public Record Office, London, England
Rev. Va.	Robert L. Scribner, *et al.*, eds., *Revolutionary Virginia...*
RG	Record Group
VMHB	*Virginia Magazine of History and Biography*
WCL	William L. Clements Library, Ann Arbor, Mich.
WHC	The State Historical Society of Wisconsin, *Collections*
WO	War Office Papers, series/volume, PRO

Fort Niagara's bakehouse, erected in 1762, produced bread for the garrison as well as for Native American delegates who visited the post to confer with Lt. Col. Caldwell.

NOTES

1. Although many works have been written about the warfare on the New York frontier during the American Revolution, no one has yet underetaken a serious, comprehensive study of Fort Niagara and its dependencies during this period. Only brief, though useful overviews are given in two recent guidebooks: Brian Leigh Dunnigan, *History and Development of Old Fort Niagara* (Youngstown, N.J.: Old Fort Niagara Association, Inc., 1985); and Brian Leigh Dunnigan, *A History and Guide to Old Fort Niagara* (Youngstown, N.Y.: Old Fort Niagara Association, Inc., 1985). Stephen G. Strach, *The British Occupation of the Niagara Frontier* (Niagara Falls, Ont.: The Lundy's Lane Historical Society, 1976) is a booklet providing a compilation of British forces serving at Niagara, 1759-1796, but only a brief account of events at the fort. Robert W. Howard, *Thundergate: The Forts of Niagara* (Englewood Cliffs, N.J.: Prentice-Hall, Inc., 1968) offers merely a sketchy, semi-popular overview. Robert B. Roberts, *New York's Forts in the Revolution* (Rutherford, Madison, and Teaneck, N.J.: Fairleigh Dickinson Unversity Press, 1980), pp. 336-362, 407-408 offers only superficial, often inaccurate information drawn from a few secondary works. Barbara Graymont, *The Iroquois in the American Revolution* (Syracuse: Syracuse University Press, 1972) simply touches upon events at Niagara in passing. At present, the most useful, though narrowly-focused, study remains Bruce G. Wilson, "The Struggle for Wealth and Power at Fort Niagara, 1775-1783," *OH*, LXVIII (Sept., 1976), 137-154

2. Despite his key role in British-Indian affairs for some forty years, John Butler still lacks a full-length biography. R. Arthur Bowler and Bruce G. Wilson, "John Butler," *DCB*, IV, 117-120 provides the most useful, well-researched, and accurate overview of Butler's life. Reliable accounts of his undeservedly notorious son are: Ernest A. Cruikshank, "Memoir of Captain Walter Butler," *Transactions of The Royal Canadian Institute (Toronto)*, IV, pt. 2 (Dec., 1895), 284-298; and David A. Charters, "Walter Butler," *DCB*, IV, 120-121. Unfortunately, Howard Swiggett, *War Out of Niagara: Walter Butler and the Tory Rangers* (New York: Columbia University Press, 1933) is so full of inaccuracies and distortions that it is best left unread. Much to be preferred are: Ernest A. Cruikshank, *The Story of Butler's Rangers and the Settlement of Niagara* (Wellend, Ont.: Lundy's Lane Historical Society, 1893); and Mary B. Fryer, *King's Men: The Soldier Founders of Ontario* (Toronto and Charlottetown: Dundurn Press Ltd., 1980), pp. 129-178. Laudatory of the Butlers but generally uninformative are: Howard Swiggett, "A Portrait of Colonel John Butler," *NYH*, XVIII (1937), 304-311; and Douglas G. Browne, "The Butlers of Butlersbury," *Cornhill Magazine*, n.s. II (Nov., 1921), 601-616.

3. The standard and most recent biography of Joseph Brant is Isabel T. Kelsay, *Joseph Brant, 1743-1807: Man of Two Worlds* (Syracuse: Syracuse University Press, 1984). It supersedes the previous standard account: William L. Stone, Sr., *Life of Joseph Brant — Thayendanegea; Including The Border Wars of the American Revolution...* (2 vols.; New York: Alexander V. Blake, 1838). All published biographies prior to Kelsay's were based almost entirely on Stone's. Brief but useful overviews of Brant's life include: Barbara Graymont, "Thayendanegea," *DCB*, V, 803-812; James H. O'Donnell, III, "Joseph Brant," in *American Indian Leaders: Studies in Diversity*, ed. R. David Edmunds (Lincoln: University of Nebraska Press, 1980), pp. 21-40; and Isabel T. Kelsay, "Joseph Brant: The Legend and the Man, A Forward," *NYH*, XL (Oct., 1959), 368-379.

4. Harley L. Gibbs, "Colonel Guy Johnson, Superintendent General of Indian Affairs, 1774-1782," *Papers of the Michigan Academy of Sciences, Arts and Letters*, XXVII (1942), 595-613; Jonathan G. Rossie, "Guy Johnson," *DCB*, IV, 393-394.

5. Frank H. Severance, "With Bolton at Niagara," in Frank H. Severance, *Old Trails on the Niagara Frontier* (2nd ed.: Cleveland: The Burrows Brothers Co., 1903), pp. 54-84 is the fullest available account, but it is not entirely free of errors. See also: James Murray Hadden, *Hadden's Journal and Orderly Books: A Journal Kept in Canada and Upon Burgoyne's Campaign in 1776 and 1777, by Lieutenant James Murray Hadden ...*, ed. Horatio Rogers (Albany: Joel Munsell's Sons, 1884), pp. 260-261, n. fg; and [Richard Cannon], *Historical Record of the King's, Liverpool Regiment of Foot, containing an Account of the Formation of the Regiment in 1685, and of its Subsequent Services to 1881; Also, Succession Lists of the Officers Who Served in Each of the Regimental Ranks, with Biographical Notices and Summaries of Their War Services* (rev. ed.; London: Harrison and Sons, 1883), p. 277.

6. App. No. 10: "Brig. Gen. Henry Watson Powell," Hadden, *Journal,* ed. Rogers, pp. 464-467; and

James P. Baxter, ed., *The British Invasion from the North: The Campaigns of Generals Carleton and Burgoyne from Canada, 1776-1777, with the Journal of Lieut. William Digby of the 53rd, or Shropshire Regiment of Foot* (Albany: Joel Munsell's Sons, 1887), pp. 196-199, n. 147.

7. George F. G. Stanley, "Allan Maclean of Torloisk," *DCB*, IV, 503-504; App. No. 21: "Brig. Gen. Allan Maclean," Hadden, *Journal*, ed. Rogers, pp. 547-555; John P. McLean, *An Historical Account of the Settlement of Scotch Highlanders in America Prior to the Peace of 1783, Together With Notice of Highland Regiments and Biographical Sketches* (Cleveland: The Helman-Taylor Co.; Glasgow: John Mackay, 1900), pp. 389-392; Fryer, *King's Men*, pp. 34-37.

8. No scholarly biography of Arent Schuyler De Peyster has yet appeared. Brief sketches of his career include: "Colonel Arent de Piester," *The Kingsman: The Journal of the King's Regiment,* III (June, 1932), 4-5; Douglas Brymner's notes on De Peyster, *MPHSC*, XX, 296-299; [Cannon], *Historical Record of the King's, Liverpool Regiment* (1883 ed.), pp. 210, 212, 215, 222, 225, 277-278; John Askin, *The John Askin Papers,* ed. Milo M. Quaife (2 vols.; Detroit: Detroit Library Commission, 1928-1931), I, 72, n. 12. His years at Michilimackinac are recounted fully in David A. Armour and Keith R. Widder, *At the Crossroads: Michilimackinac during the American Revolution* (Mackinac Island, Mich.: Mackinac Island State Park Commission, 1978). De Peyster tells of some of his American adventures in verse in Arent S. De Peyster, *Miscellanies, by an Officer* (Dumfries, Scotland: C. Munro, at the Dumfries and Galloway Courier Office, 1813; republished, ed. with app. and notes by J. Watts de Peyster, New York: C. H. Ludwig, 1888).

9. Paul R. Reynolds, *Guy Carleton: A Biography* (New York: William Morrow and Co., Inc., 1980), pp. xi-xii; Paul H. Smith, "Sir Guy Carleton: Soldier-Statesman," *George Washington's Opponents: British Generals and Admirals in the American Revolution,* ed. George A. Billias (New York: William Morrow and Co., Inc., 1969), p. 105.

10. There is no existing biographical sketch of this John Caldwell. The outlines of his military career can be found in: [Cannon], *Historical Record of the King's, Liverpool Regiment* (1883 ed.), pp. 210, 277; Richard Cannon, *Historical Record of the Seventh Regiment, or The Royal Fusiliers; containing An Account of the Formation of the Regiment in 1685, and of Its Subsequent Services to 1846* (London: Parker, Furnival, & Parker, 1847), p. 24; and *NYCD*, VIII, 509 n. 1. His family connections can be traced in several articles regarding his younger brother Henry and his nephew John: "La Famille Caldwell," *Le Bulletin des recherches historiques,* XLII (Jan. 1936), 3-6; Marcel Caya, "Henry Caldwell," *DCB*, V, 130-133; David Boston, "The Three Caldwells," *The Kingsman: The Journal of the King's Regiment,* n.s. III (Dec., 1963), 316-317. See also John Bernard Burke, *A Genealogical and Heraldic Dictionary of the Peerage and Baronetage of the British Empire* (17th ed.; London: Hurst and Blackett, 1855), p. 153.

The Caldwell Family Papers in the Bagshawe Muniments at the John Rylands University Library of Manchester, England, contain a few letters from or about John Caldwell. Unfortunateley, these are generally uninformative about his military life. Those pertinent to his early career are: [Maj.] John Caldwell to Lady [Elizabeth] Caldwell [his sister-in-law], Fort George, North Britain, Sept. 17, 1768, B3/29/94; Maj. J[ohn] C[aldwell] to "My Dear Brother" [Sir James Caldwell], n.p. [Chatham, Eng.], June 13, 1772, B3/13/84; Maj. J[ohn] C[aldwell] to Sir James Caldwell, London, June 28, 1772, B3/13/85; Col. J[ohn] C[aldwell] to Sir James Caldwell, Bath, Jan. 7, 1773, B3/13/86; and [nephew] John Caldwell to Lady [Elizabeth] Caldwell (his mother), Bromley, Dec. 26, 1770, B3/29/108.

11. Earl of Hillsborough to William, Viscount Barrington, Whitehall, Feb. 20, 1768, HMC, *The Manuscripts of the Earl of Dartmouth (3 vols.; London: Her Majesty's Stationery Office, 1887-1896), II, 555;* Gen. Thomas Gage to Barrington, New York, Aug. 20, 1768, and Apr. 13, 1772, *Gage Corr.*, II, 482, 601; Capt. Francis Hutcheson, General Return of the Number of Rations of Provisions Issued to His Majesty's Troops in North America ... between the 25th June and 24th December 1772, HP/BL Add. MSS. 21,694, fol. 26; Distribution of His Majesty's Forces in North America, July 5, 1773, HP/BL Add. MSS. 21,696, fol. 25; [Cannon], *Historical Record of the King's, Liverpool Regiment* (1883 ed.), p. 268, Cannon, *Historical Record of the Seventh Regiment,* p. 24; Caya, "Henry Caldwell," *DCB*, V, 130-133; "La Famille Caldwell," pp. 3-6; George F. G. Stanley, *Canada Invaded, 1775-1776* (Toronto and Sarasota: Samuel Stevens, Hakkert & Co., 1977), p. 78. See also the possible reference to Lieutenant Colonel Caldwell's presence in Dublin in June, 1773, in John Caldwell to Lady [Elizabeth] Caldwell (his mother), Dublin Castle, June 8, 1773, B3/29/109, Caldwell Family Papers, Bagshawe Muniments, JRUL..

12. Randolph C. Downes, *Council Fires on the Upper Ohio: A Narrative of Indian Affairs in the Upper Ohio Valley until 1795* (Pittsburgh: University of Pittsburgh Press, 1940), p. 132; Jack M. Sosin, *The Revolutionary Frontier, 1763-1783* (New York: Holt, Rinehart and Winston, 1967), pp. 13-16; Nelson V. Russell, *The British Régime in Michigan and the Old Northwest, 1760-1796* (Northfield, Minn.: Carleton College, 1939), pp. 52, 123, 162-163; Gage to Gen. Frederick Haldimand, New York, June 3, 1773, HP/Bl Add. MSS. 21,665, fols. 131-132.

13. Haldimand to Maj. Henry Bassett, to Lt. Col. Francis Smith, and to Capt. John Vattas, New York, Dec. 26, 1773, HP/BL Add. MSS. 2 1,693, fols. 281-285; Haldimand to Capt. Gabriel Maturin, New York, Feb. 18, and Apr. 19, 1774, HP/Bl ADD MSS. 21,693, fols. 323-324, 375; Lt. Col. Valentine Jones to Haldimand, Quebec, Mar. 24, 1774, HP/BL Add. MSS. 21,731, fol. 95; Ens. Durell Saumarez to Thomas Saumarez, Niagara, Apr. 10, 1777, Durell Saumarez Papers, MG 23, K10, I, 1-4; PAC; Edward E. Curtis, *The Organization of the British Army in the American Revovlution* (New Haven: Yale University Press, 1926), pp. 3-6, 150; William L. Potter, "Redcoats on the Frontier: The King's Regiment in the Revolutionary War," pp. 41-60 in *Selected Papers from the 1983 and 1984 George Rogers Clark Trans-Appalachian Frontier History Conferences,* ed. Roberet Holden (Vincenenes, Ind.: Eastern National Park and Monument Associaton, 1985).

Strength and distribution of the 8th Regiment are found in: Distribution of IIis Majesty's Forces in North America, 19th July 1775, *Gage Corr.,* II, 690-691; and Distribution of the 8th Rgt at the Upper Posts prior to the War of the Revolution, n.d. [prob. 1785], HP/*MPHSC*, XX, 272. Sylvia R. Frey, *The British Soldier in America: A Social History of Military Life in the Revolutionary Period* (Austin: University of Texas Press, 1981), p. 24, table 5 gives a brief statistical analysis of the experience, age, and size of the soldiers of the 8th Regiment, drawn from War Office returns of 1782.

14. Haldimand to Maturin, New York, Feb. 18, and Apr. 19, 1774. HP/ BL Add. MSS. 21,693 fols. 323-324, 375; Haldimand, Instructions for the Commanding Officers of the First Division and of the Second Division of the Eighth or Kings Regiment ..., New York, Feb. 26, 1774, HP/BL Add. MSS. 21,693, fols. 349-352; V. Jones to Haldimand, Quebec, Mar. 24, 1774, HP/BL Add. MSS. 21,731, fol. 95; Lt. Col. Dudley Templer to Haldimand, Montreal, May 22, 1774, HP/*MPHSC*, XIX, 316-317.

15. V. Jones to Haldimand, Quebec, Mar. 24, 1774, HP/BL Add. MSS. 21,731, fol. 95; Templer to Haldimand, Montreal, May 22, 1774, HP/*MPHSC*, XIX, 316-317; Bassett to Capt. Thomas Moncrieffe and to Haldimand, Detroit, July 3, 1774, and Capt. Richard B. Lernoult's Receipt, Detroit, July 6, 1774, Thomas Gage Papers, American series, vol. 120, WCL; Vattas to Haldimand, Michilimackinac, July 13, 1774, encl. Return of Indian Goods Left at Michilimackinac by Capt. Vatta of the Tenth Regimt. of Foot, July 12, 1774, and Capt. Arent S. De Peyster to Haldimand, Michilimackinac, July 16, 1774, Gage Papers, Am. sr., vol. 121, WCL; [Cannon], *Historical Record of the King's, Liverpool Regiment* (1883 ed.), pp. 12, 215; *British Army List* (1774), p. 62.

16. Lt. Col. John Caldwell to [Haldimand], Montreal, June 5, 1774, and Niagara, Aug. 7, 1774, Gage Papers, Am. ser., vols. 19 and 122, WCL; Capt. George Forster to Gage, Oswegatchie, Aug. 10, 1774, Gage Papers, Am. ser., vol. 122, WCL; Haldimand to Maturin, New York, Feb. 18, 1774, HP/BL Add. MSS. 1,693, fols. 323-324; V. Jones to Haldimand, Quebec, Mar. 24, 1774, HP/BL Add. MSS. 21,731, fol. 95.

17. No sooner had the 10th Regiment reassembled at Quebec in September, 1774, than Governor Carleton dispatched it and the 52nd Regiment to join General Gage's garrison at Boston. When Gage decided in April, 1775, to send an expeditionary force to seize colonial military stores and leaders at Lexington and Concord, he entrusted the detacment's command to Lieutenant Colonel Smith. Not long after the debacle of April 19, Smith returned ot England, where he was appointed one of the military aides-de-camp to King George III. In this capacity in 1777 the former Niagara commandant helped the ministry plan for the employment of the Six Nations Indians in the ensuing campaigns in New York.

18. Niagara's Revolutionary-era fortifications, dependent posts, and garrison are described in: Francis Grant, "Journal from New York to Canada, 1767," *NYH,* XIII (Apr.-July, 1932), 191-193; John Porteous to his father, Michilimackinac, Aug. 16, 1767, "From Niagara to Mackinac in 1767," ed. F. Clever Bald, *Algonquin Club* [of Detroit] *Historical Bulletin,* no. 2 (Mar., 1938), 5-7; Caldwell to Gage, Niagara, Sept. 11, and Nov. 15, 1774, Gage Papers, Am. ser., vols. 123 and 124, WCL; [Paul Long] to George Morgan, Pittsburgh, July 23, 1776, GMLB 1776, pp. 43-49, PHMC; Ens. Durell Saumarez to Thomas Saumarez, Niagara, Apr. 10, 1777, Durell Saumarez Papers, MG 23, K10, I, 1-4, PAC; Month-

ly Return of the Garrison of Niagara and its dependencies, May 1, 1778, HP/BL Add. MSS. 21,833, fol. 12; Lt. Col. Mason Bolton to Haldimand, Niagara, Sept. 18, 1778, HP/BL Add. MSS. 21,756, fol. 65; Bolton to Haldimand, Niagara, Mar. 4, 1779, HP/BL Add. MSS. 21,760, fols. 96-97; Gen. George Washington, Summary of Intelligence concerning the planned expedition against the Six Nations, n.d. [ca. Apr., 1779], Maryly B. Penrose, comp., *Indian Affairs Papers: American Revolution* (Franklin Park, N.J.: Liberty Bell Associates, 1981), pp. 207-209; Bolton, State of six Companies of the King's (or 8th) Regiment of Foot, in Garrison at Niagara, &ca., May 21, 1779, HP/BL Add. MSS. 21,760, fol. 128; Charles G. DeWitt, "The Captivity of Capt. Jeremiah Snyder & Elias Snyder, of Saugerties, Ulster Co., N.Y." *Saugerties Telegraph*, V. nos. 13 and 14, Jan. 25, and Feb. 1, 1851 (facsim. New York and London: Garland Publishing, Inc., 1977), no pagination; John Enys, *The American Journals of John Enys*, ed. Elizabeth Cometti (Syracuse: Adirondack Museum and Syracuse University Press, 1976), pp. 144-146; Isaac Weld, Jr., *Travels Through the States of North America, and the Provinces of Upper and Lower Canada, during the Years 1795, 1796, and 1797* (London: John Stockdale, 1799), p. 300; [John Lees], *Journal of J. L., of Quebec, Merchant*, ed. M. Agnes Burton (Detroit: Society of Colonial Wars of the State of Michigan, 1911), p. 27, n. 52; Howard, *Thundergate*, pp. 107-115; Dunnigan, *History and Development of Old Fort Niagara*, pp. 5-7, 25-26; Dunnigan, *A History and Guide to Old Fort Niagara*, pp. 12, 29-71. [Francois Alexander Frederic], duc de La Rochefoucault Liancourt, *Travels through the United States of North America, the Country of the Iroquois, and Upper Canada, in the Years 1795, 1796, and 1797*, trans. Henry Neuman (2 vols.; London: T. Davison, 1799), I, 214 offers a 1795 description of Fort Erie, largely unchanged after twenty years.

19. See Brian Leigh Dunnigan, *Siege—1759: The Campaign Against Niagara* (Youngstown, N.Y.: Old Fort Niagara Association, Inc., 1986).

20. Apparently there is no extant plan or map of Fort Niagara dating specifically from the years of Colonel Caldwell's tenure. The post's outlines at the time of Caldwell's arrival can readily be discovered, however, in two detailed plans prepared by Lieutenant Francis Pfister: "Plan of Niagara," 1771, WCL; and "Plan of Niagara with an Explanation of its present State," Sept. 28, 1773, Crown Maps, cxxi, 76, British Library. Two other existing plans probably date from the later years of the American Revolution. One is an undated plan (probably ca. 1780) found in the PRO (MPH 275), and the other is John Luke, "Fort Niagara," n.d. [ca. 1781-1782], John Bradstreet Papers, American Antiquarian Society, Worcester, Mass. (a primitive plan possibly drawn by an American prisoner held at the fort during the command of General Henry Watson Powell). The first, second, and fourth of the above are discussed in Dunnigan, *History and Development of Old Fort Niagara*, pp. 25-25, 47-48. Also of great interest is "The Fort of Niagara as commanded together with the whole Upper District of Canada By Col. D. P. in 1784-& 85," Item 3, Collection of Papers Relating to Col. A. S. de Peyster, Ewart Public Library, Dumfries, Scotland. This small sketch seems to have been copied from one of Pfister's plans, but it is significant for showing the buildings situated in the "Bottoms" beside the river at the close of the Revolution. It also indicates that the British preserved through all or most of the war years the interior stockade constructed around the "Castle" and several barracks buildings, a measure taken in 1768 to provide a manageable defensive perimeter for the small British garrison and a peacetime refuge from the swarms of Indians and traders who frequented Niagara.

21. For the state of the naval department and other shipping on the Great Lakes during the early years of the American Revolution, see: Earl of Hillsborough to Gage, Whitehall Apr. 15, 1768, and Gage to Hillsborough, New York, June 4, 1771, *Gage Corr.*, II, 61-66, and I, 299-301; Caldwell to Gage, Niagara, Aug. 14, Sept. 15, and Nov. 2, 1774, Gage Papers, Am. ser., vols. 122, 23, 124, WCL; A Return of the shipping on the Lakes Ontario, Erie and Huron, June 12, 1775, as printed in Perry E. LeRoy, "Sir Guy Carleton as a Military Leader during the American Invasion and Repulse in Canada, 1775-1776; ; (Ph.D. dissertation, Ohio State University, 1960), pp. 624-625; Information regarding Detroit [an unsigned letter], Detroit, Apr. 2, 1776, Reuben G. Thwaites and Louise P. Kellogg, eds., *The Revolution on the Upper Ohio, 1775-1777* (Madison: The State Historical Society of Wisconsin, 1908), pp. 147-151; Return of H.M.'s three vessels and five private vessels on Lakes Ontario, Erie and Huron, under command of Capt. Alexander Grant, Detroit, Aug. 2, 1776, *DAR*, X, 346, #1918; Return of all the Vessels upon Lake George, Champlain, Ontario, Erie, Huron & Michigan, &c. From the year 1759 till this date, Excepting those employed at present upon Lake Champlain, Quebec, July 30, 1778, *WHC*, XI, 198-199; Alexander Grant, A General Return of the Force & Burthen of His Majesty's Armed Vessels, etc., on Lake Erie, Huron & Michigan, Detroit, Aug. 1, 1782, HP/*MPHSC*, X, 618; Milo M. Quaife, "Commodore Alexander Grant," *BHCL*, VI, no. 5 (1928); George F. Macdonald, "Commodore Grant," Ontario Historical Society, *Papers and Records*, XXII (1925), 167-181; K. R. Macpherson, "List of Vessels Employed on British Naval Service on the Great Lakes, 1755-1875," *OH*, LV

(Sept., 1963), 172-179; Armour and Widder, *At the Crossroads,* pp. 65-66; Russell, *British Régime,* pp. 169-175.

22. Hillsborough to Gage, Whitehall, May 4, 1771, and Han[over] Square, May 4, 1771 (private), *Gage Cor.,* II, 129-130, 130-131; Gage to Hillsborough, New York, July 2, 1771 (private), and July 2, 1771, and Gage to Barrington, New York, July 2, 1771, *Gage Cor.,* I, 301-302, 302-303, and II, 582; Pierce Sinnott to John Pownall, London, Apr. 20, 1774, HMC, *Dartmouth Manuscripts,* II, 565; Gage to John Robinson, [London], Apr. 1, 1776, and Robinson to Gen. William Howe, Treasury Chambers, Aug. 6, 1777, and Howe to Robinson, Philadelphia, Dec. 13, 1777, and Power of Attorney of Lt. Gov. Pierce Sinnott, Apr. 23, 1779, and Gen. Guy Carleton, Warrant for the pay of Pierce Sinnott, New York, Dec. 19, 1782, and Sinnott to Carleton, London, Mar. 5, 1783, Headquarters Papers of the British Army in America, #149, 642, 804, 1,949, 6,449, and 10,068, PRO 30/55, PRO; John R. Alden, *John Stuart and the Southern Colonial Frontier* (Ann Arbor: The University of Michigan Press, 1944), pp. 202-203, and 203, n. 53; Helen L. Shaw, *British Administration of the Southern Indians, 1756-1783* (Lancaster, Pa.: Lancaster Press, Inc., 1931), pp. 175-177.

23. This description of the place of Niagara and its commandant in the British west of 1774 derives from the author's reading of all the extant official correspondence to and from Niagara and the other frontier posts, 1774-1783. Regarding communications and Fort Ontario, see Caldwell to Gage, Niagara, Aug. 14, and Sept. 4, 1774, Gage Papers, Am. ser., vols. 122 and 123, WCL. That the governor of Quebec regarded Niagara's commandant as commandant over the other upper posts as well is stated plainly in Haldimand to Bolton, Quebec, Sept. 12,1780, HP/BL Add. MSS. 21,764, fols. 144-145. The quotation is from Caldwell to Lady [Elizabeth] Caldwell, Niagara, Nov. 1, 1774, B3/29/95, Caldwell Family Papers, Bagshawe Muniments, JRUL.

24. Caldwell to Guy Johnson, Niagara, Sept. 29, 1774, *NYCD,* VIII, 509.

25. The Indian service at Niagara at the time of Colonel Caldwell's arrival is detailed in: F. Smith to Maturin, Niagara, June 29, 1773, HP/BL Add. MSS. 1,730, fol. 107; Haldimand to Smith, New York, Aug. 18, and Dec. 26, 1773, HP/BL Add. MSS. 1,693, fols. 126 and 283-284; Phyn & Ellice to Edward Pollard, Schenectady, July 17, 1774, Phyn & Ellice LB, III, 108; B&ECHS; Caldwell to Maturin, Niagara, Dec. 5, 1774, Gage Papers, Am. ser., vol. 24, WCL; Return of Officers and other appointments of the Northern Department of Indian Affairs on the Peace Establishment previous to the late Rebellion in America, Montreal, Dec. 10, 1783, HP/BL Add. MSS. 21,882, fol. 54.

26. Jean-Baptiste De Couagne (baptized 1720; died after 1795) was losing his health and eyesight in 1774. By then he had already led an extraordinarily eventful life in the Indian trade in Illinois and in New York. In 1772 he sent one son to school in Schenectady. Another son became principal chief of the Kaskaskia Indians in Illinois. See: Jane E. Graham, "Jean-Baptiste De Couagne," *DCB,* IV, 173-174; Henry Hamilton to Haldimand, Detroit, Oct. 7, 1778, HP/*MPHSC,* IX, 486-487; "The King's Shipyard," *BHCL,* II, no. 3 (Jan., 1924), 25; and Donald H. Kent and Merle H. Deardorff, eds., "John Adlum on the Allegheny: Memoir of the Year 1794," *PMHB,* LXXXIV (1960), 444, n. 1.

27. Edward Pollard was certainly the wiliest and probably the most successful of Niagara's British merchants. References to him abound in the correspondence of the period (especially in the Phyn & Ellice LB, B&ECHS), and his career deserves more careful examination. The specific references here are: "The King's Shipyard," p. 25; Bolton to Haldimand, Niagara, Sept. 4, 1778, WO 28/2, fol. 206; PRO; Commissary Daniel Bliss to Brig. Henry Watson Powell, Niagara, Sept. 30, 1782, HP/BL Add. MSS. 21,761, fols. 182-184; William Ketchum, *An Authentic and Comprehensive History of Buffalo* ... (2 vols.; Buffalo: Rockwell, Baker & Hill, 1864-1865), II, 123; Oscar J. Harvey, *A History of Wilkes-Barre, Luzerne County, Pennsylvania* ... (3 vols.; Wilkes Barré: Raeder Press, 1909), II, 1,041-1,042.

28. Useful information about Seneca culture and history and about the Seneca's place in the Six Nations Confederacy is found in: William C. Sturtevant, ed., *Handbook of North American Indians* (20 vols.; Washington, D.C.: Smithsonian Institution, 1978-), vol. XV, *Northeast,* ed. Bruce G. Trigger (1978), pp. 505-517; Lewis Henry Morgan, *League of the Ho-de'-no-sau-nee, Iroquois* (1851; republished Secaucus, N.J.: The Citadel Press, 1972); Anthony F.C. Wallace, with Shelia C. Steen, *The Death and Rebirth of the Seneca* (New York: Alfred A. Knopf, 1970); Col. [Daniel] Claus's Remarks on the Management of the Northern Indian Nations, [London, Mar. 1, 1777], *NYCS,* VIII, 700-704; and Guy Johnson's Map of the Country of the VI. Nations, 1771, Edmund B. O'Callaghan, ed., *The Doc-*

mentary History of the State of New-York (4 vols.; Albany: Weed, Parsons & Co., 1849-1851), IV, following 660. The description of the Senecas given here, however, is drawn from the much fuller and heavily-documented account of the Six Nations Confederacy and its constituent tribes given in Paul L. Stevens, "His Majesty's 'Savage' Allies: British Policy and the Northern Indians during the Revolutionary War—The Carleton Years, 1774-1778" (Ph.D. dissertation, State University of New York at Buffalo, 1984), pp. 71-81, 116. The 1774 population of the Six Nations, including the Senecas, together with the numerous relevant primary sources, are discussed in detail in *ibid.,* pp. 73-74, 76, and 1,871-1,873, n. 7. See also Graymont, *Iroquois in Revolution,* pp. 1-25.

29. Donald B. Smith, "Who are the Mississauga?" *OH,* LXVII (Dec., 1975), 211-222; Donald B. Smith, "The Dispossession of the Mississauga Indians: A Missing Chapter in the Early History of Upper Canada," *OH,* LXXIII (June, 1981), 67-87; Sturtevant, ed., *Handbook,* XV, 760-771; Robert Hunter, Jr., *Quebec to Carolina in 1785-1786: Being the Travel Diary and Observations of Robert Hunter, Jr., a Young Merchant of London,* ed. Louis B. Wright and Marion Tinling (San Marino, Calif.: The Huntington Library, 1943), p. 97; Patrick Campbell, *Travels in the Interior Inhabited Parts of North America in the Years 1791 and 1792,* ed. H. H. Langton (Edinburgh, 1793; republished Toronto: The Champlain Society, 1937), p. 158; Weld, *Travels during 1795, 1796, and 1797,* pp. 294, 376; Ernest A. Cruikshank, ed., "The Journal of Capt. Walter Butler on a Voyage along the North Shore of Lake Ontario from the 8th to the 16th of March, 1779," *Transactions of the Royal Canadian Institute (Toronto),* IV, pt. 1 (1892-93), 279-293; Wilbur H. Siebert, "The Loyalists and the Six Nation Indians in the Niagara Peninsula," *Transactions of the Royal Society of Canada,* 3rd ser., IX (1915), 79.

30. Caldwell to [Gage], Niagara, Aug. 7 and 14, 1774, Gage Papers, Am. ser., vol. 122, WCL; De Peyster to Haldimand, Michilimackinac, July 16, 1774, and Lernoult to Haldimand, Fort Detroit, Aug. 1, 1774, and Forster to Gage, Oswegatchie, Aug. 10, 1774, Gage Papers, Am. ser., vols. 121 and 122, WCL; Lt. Henry Du Vernet (R.R.A.) to Lt. Col. Samuel Cleaveland (R.R.A.), Niagara, Sept. 4, and Nov. 5, 1774, and Aug. 1, 1775, WO 55/1537, fols. 17, 119, and 132, PRO; Gage to Caldwell, Boston, Oct. 5, 1774, HP/BL Add. MSS. 1,678, fol. 189; Monthly Return of the Garrison of Niagara and its dependencies, May 1, 1778, HP/Bl Add. MSS. 21,833, fol. 12; Bolton to Haldimand, Niagara, Sept. 18, 1778, HP/BL Add. MSS. 21,756, fol. 5.

31. The Royal American Regiment recruited its rank and file and many of its junior officers in the colonies, so it is likely that Potts was American-born. For his arrival at Niagara, see: Haldimand to Caldwell, New York, July 26, 1774, HP/BL Add. MSS. 1,693, fol. 465; and Caldwell to Gage, Niagara, Sept. 15, 1774, Gage Papers, Am. ser., vol. 123, WCL. For his military background, see: Gage to Welbore Ellis, New York, Apr. 26, 1765, *Gage Cor.,* II, 282; *British Army List* (1774), p. 62; Ens. Walter Butler to Charles de Langlade Fort Erie, Nov. 16, 1776, *WHC,* XVIII, 356, and also 356, n. 74; Joseph Hadfield, *An Englishman in America, 1785: Being the Diary of Joseph Hadfield,* ed. Douglas S. Robertson (Toronto: The Hunter-Rose Co., Ltd., 1933), p. 129 (entry for Aug. 4, 1785); Worthington C. Ford, comp., *British Officers Serving in America, 1754-1774* (Boston: Historical Printing Club, 1894), p. 83; Worthington C. Ford, comp., *British Officers Serving in the American Revolution, 1774-1783* (Brooklyn: Historical Printing Club, 1897), p. 146; [Cannon], *Historical Record of the King's, Liverpool Regiment* (1883 ed.), pp. 212, 215, 222, 225.

32. Young Ensign Caldwell was transferred to the garrison at Detroit sometime during 1775. For his 1774 arrival at Niagara, see: John Caldwell, Bond and Bill for money borrowed by his father to purchase a commission for him, May 30, 1774, B3/39/1, and Gen. Bigoe Armstrong to Sir James Caldwell, London, May 18, 1774, B3/16/10, and Lt. Col. John Caldwell to Lady [Elizabeth] Caldwell, Niagara, Nov. 1, 1774, B3/29/95, Caldwell Family Papers, Bagshawe Muniments, JRUL. For his background, see Boston, "The Three Caldwells," pp. 316-317. For his career in the 8th Regiment, see [Cannon], *Historical Record of the King's, Liverpool Regiment* (1883 ed.), pp. 226, 239.

33. This account of the early stages of Dunmore's War is drawn from the detailed narrative of the activities of both British officials and Indian leaders as given in Stevens, "His Majesty's 'Savage' Allies," pp. 152-250. For convenient, brief, and fairly reliable accounts of this frontier war, see: Downes, *Council Fires on the Upper Ohio,* pp. 152-164; Robert L. Kerby, "The Other War in 1774: Dunmore's War," *West Virgnia History,* XXXVI (Oct., 1974), 1-16; Randolph C. Downes, "Dunmore's War: An Interpretation," *MVHR,* XXI (Dec., 1934), 311-330. An especially useful study, although it overlooks the key roles played by Colonel Caldwell at Niagara and Captain Lernoult at Detroit, is Jack M. Sosin, "The British Indian Department and Dunmore's War," *VMHB,* LXXIV

(Jan., 1966), 34-50. For Lernoult's role, see Paul L. Stevens, "The Indian Diplomacy of Capt. Richard B. Lernoult, British Military Commandant of Detroit, 1774-1775," *The Michigan Historical Review,* XIII (Spring, 1987), 53-63. Orders for Caldwell to cooperate with Guy Johnson were given in Gage Circular Letter to Officers commanding at Niagara, Detroit, and Missilimackinac, Salem, July 25, 1774, Gage Papers Am. ser., vol. 121, WCL.

34. Caldwell to Gage, Niagara, Aug. 14, Sept. 11, 15, and 29, 1774, Gage Papers, Am. ser., vols. 122 and 123, WCL; Caldwell to Guy Johnson, Niagara, Sept. 29, 1774, *NYCD,* VIII, 507-509.

35. Caldwell to Gage, Niagara, Sept. 29, 1774, encl. a report of Indian Intelligence about M. Sang Blanc, Gage Papers Am. ser., vol. 123, WCL; Caldwell to Guy Johnson, Niagara, Sept. 29, 1774, with a report of a French axe-belt sent to the Indians, *NYCD,* VIII, 507-509, 507; Haldimand to Caldwell, New York, July 26, 1774, HP/BL Add. MSS. 1,693, fol. 465; Gage to Caldwell, Boston, Oct. 5, 1774, HP/BL Add. MSS. 1,678, fl. 189. For the identity of Sciawa, see: *JP,* VII, 483-485, 985-987, and VIII, 17; Caldwell to Gage, Niagara, Feb. 11, 1775, Gage Papers, Am. ser., vol. 26, WCL; Carleton to Bolton, Quebec, Sept. 16, 1777, HP/BL Add. MSS. 21,700, p. 5; Richard Cartwright, Jr., Continuation of a Journal of an Expedition into the Indian Country (June-August, 1779), entry for July 12, 1779, Draper MSS., 6F48(8).

36. Caldwell to Lady [Elizabeth] Caldwell, Niagara, Nov. 1, 1774, B3/29/95, Caldwell Family Papers, Bagshawe Muniments, JRUL; Stevens, "His Majesty's 'Savage' Allies," pp. 225-250; Graymont, *Iroquois in Revolution,* pp. 50-55.

37. Caldwell to Gage, Niagara, Nov. 2, 1774, and Caldwell to Maturin, Niagara, Dec. 5, 1775, and Gage to Caldwell and to De Peyster, Boston, Oct. 5, 1774, and Gage to Lernoult, Boston, Nov. 14, 1774, Gage Papers, Am. ser., vols. 123 and 124, WCL; Gage to Dartmouth, Boston, Nov. 14, 1774, *Gage Cor.,* I, 383-384; Du Vernet to Cleaveland, Niagara, Nov. 4, 1774; WO 55/1537, fol. 119, PRO; Gage to Guy Johnson, to John Stuart, to Caldwell, to Lernoult, and to Capt. Hugh Lord, Boston, Dec. 28, 1774, Gage Papers, Am. ser., vol. 25, WCL (letter to Johnson also in *JP,* XIII, 703-704); Stevens, "Indian Diplomacy of Capt. Lernoult", pp. 64-65; Stevens, "His Majesty's 'Savage' Allies," pp. 262-276. Gage's letter to Carleton is not in the Gage Papers or Colonial Office Papers, but Carleton, in his reply, states that it was dated December 25, 1774, and made mention of the Canadians and Indians. See Carleton to Gage, Quebec, Feb. 4, 1775 (secret), *DRCHC,* I, 450-452.

38. Caldwell to Gage, Niagara, Sept. 29, 1774, and Feb. 1, and May 5, 1775, Gage Papers, Am. ser., vols. 123, 126, and 128, WCL; Phyn & Ellice to William Edgar, Schenectady, Jan. 4, 1775, Phyn & Ellice LB, III, 173, B&ECHS. See also Gage to Carleton, Boston, Aug. 18, 1775, Gage Papers Am. ser., vol. 134, WCL. The important Lower Seneca war chief Adongot (also Anandageghte and other variant spellings) resided at the village of Karaghiyadirha on the upper Genesee River and had been a leader of the Seneca warriors who had massacred British teamsters and soldiers at Devil's Hole along the Niagara portage in September, 1763; see: *JP,* VII, 1,045-1,046, VIII, 255, X, 893, and XII, 389; and Guy Johnson, Minutes of Indian Affairs 1779-1780, Mar. 1, 1780, RG 10, vol. 1830, 201, PAC.

39. Gage to Guy Johnson, Boston, Feb. 5, and Mar. 10, 1775, and to Caldwell, Boston, Mar. 4, 1775, Gage Papers, Am. ser., vols. 125 and 126, WCL; Gage to Dartmouth, Boston, Mar. 4, 1775, *Gage Cor.,* I, 393-394. For Johnson's dealings with the Iroquois during January-May, 1775, see: Graymont, *Iroquois in Revolution,* pp. 55-64; and Stevens, "His Majesty's 'Savage' Allies," pp. 278-305.

40. Caldwell to Gage, Niagara, May 1 and 5, 1775, Gage Papers Am. ser., vol. 128, WCL.

41. Stevens, "His Majesty's 'Savage' Allies," pp. 292-306; and Graymont, *Iroquois in Revolution,* pp. 62-64.

42. Guy Johnson to Haldimand, Montreal, Jan. 11, 1783, HP/BL Add. MSS. 21,768, fols. 127-128. Gage's letter to Johnson is not extant, but it must have closely paralleled his letter to Caldwell. Moreover, Gage enclosed in a letter to Carleton an extract of the brief paragraph containing his orders to the superintendent. See: Gage to Carleton, Boston, May 20, 1775, encl. an extract of a letter from Gage to Guy Johnson, Boston, May 10, 1775, and Gage to Caldwell, Boston, May 10, 1775, Gage Papers Am. ser., vols. 128 and 129, WCL.

43. Gage to Carleton, Boston, Apr. 21 and 27, 1775, Gage Papers, Am. ser. vols. 127 and 128, WCL;

Gage to Carleton, to Caldwell, to Lernoult, and to De Peyster, Boston, May 20, 1775, and Carleton to Gage, Montreal, June 28, 1775, Gage Papers, Am. ser., vols. 129 and 130, WCL. All aspects of General Gage's role in ordering the British employment of the Indians in 1775 are discussed and documented in Stevens, "His Majesty's 'Savage' Allies," pp. 305-312, and 1,965-1,967, nn. 30-35. See also: Jack M. Sosin, "The Use of Indians in the War of the American Revolution: A Re-Assessment of Responsibility," *CHR*, XLVI (June, 1965), 101-121; John R. Alden, *General Gage in America* (Baton Rouge: Louisiana State University Press, 1948), pp. 256-263.

44. The story of the withdrawal of Guy Johnson and the Indian Department from the Mohawk Valley and the council with the Six Nations at Oswego is told and documented in detail in Stevens, "His Majesty's 'Savage' Allies," pp. 328-340 and 1,973-1,980, nn. 53-61. See also Graymont, *Iroquois in Revolution*, pp. 64-66. For the place of Colonel Caldwell, Governor Carleton, and Niagara in these events, see particularly: Journal of Colonel Guy Johnson from May to November, 1775, *NYCD*, VIII, 658-659; Gage to Caldwell, Boston, May 10 and 20, 1775, and Carleton to Gage, Montreal, June 28, and July 27, 1775, Gage Papers Am. ser., vols. 128, 129, 130, and 132, WCL; Carleton to Dartmouth, Montreal, June 26, 1775, CO 42/34, fols. 155-156, PRO; Phyn & Ellice to Pollard, Schenectady, June 13, 1775, to John Porteous (at Niagara), June 21, 1775, and to James Sterling (at Detroit), June 22, 1775, Phyn & Ellice LB, III, 205-206, 208-209, 209-210, B&ECHS; Affidavit of Benjamin Davis alias John Johnson, Albany, Aug. 8, 1775, Penrose, comp., *Indian Affairs Papers*, pp. 4-5.

45. In 1774 Captain Lernoult garrisoned Detroit with three companies (about 120 rank and file). Subsequently, rebel spies reported that Detroit had only "Seventy good Soldiers" (two companies) circa July-August, 1775, but "120 Soldiers" (three companies) in March, 1776. This implies that one of Detroit's companies spent July-October, 1775, elsewhere. Caldwell's threatened posts on the Niagara Frontier seem the most likely place. See: Matthew Elliott to the Gentlemen of the West Augusta Committee of Safety, n.p., n.d. (received Aug. 23, 1775, delivered by John Gibson to James Wilson at Pittsburgh), *Rev. Va.*, IV, 451 and Information regarding Detroit [an unsigned letter], Detroit, Apr. 2, 1776, Thwaites and Kellogg, eds., *Rev. on Upper Ohio*, pp. 147-151.

46. Stevens, "His Majesty's 'Savage' Allies," pp. 361-486. See also: Graymont, *Iroquois in Revolution*, pp. 65-85; James F. Vivian and Jean N. Vivian, "Congressional Indian Policy during the War for Independence: The Northern Department," *Maryland Historical Magazine*, LXIII (Sept., 1968), 241-274; Downes, *Council Fires on the Upper Ohio*, pp. 179-189; Gustave Linctot, *Canada and the American Revolution, 1774-1783*, trans. Margaret M. Cameron (Cambridge: Harvard University Press, 1967), pp. 43-107; Stanley, *Canada Invaded*, pp. 3-70.

47. Gage to Caldwell, Boston, May 20, 1775, Gage Papers, Am. ser., vol. 129, WCL; Account of Bills drawn from the Posts in the Upper Country paid by Thomas Dunn Esqr. in 1775 by order of Gen. Guy Carleton, HP/*MPHSC*, XX, 205; Report of the Indian Commissioners anent Information Received from the Doctor through Simon Girty, [Pittsburgh], Sept. 20, 1775, *Rev. Va.*, IV, 129-130; the same as Information from the Allegheny Senecas, reported by The Doctor [Mohawk], Pittsburgh, Sept. 20, 1775, Thwaites and Kellogg, eds., *Rev. on Upper Ohio*, pp. 67-70; Adam Stephen to Richard Henry Lee, Pittsburgh, Sept. 23, 1775, *Am. Arch.*, 4-111, 776-777; Simon Girty's report to George Morgan, Pittsburgh, July 26, 1776, GMLB 1776, p. 53, PHMC.

48. For Caldwell's work parties, see Du Vernet to Cleaveland, Niagara, Aug. 11, 1775, WO 55/1537, fol. 132, PRO. The exact date of the *Caldwell*'s launch remains problematic. It is given as 1774 in Return of all the Vessels upon Lake George, Champlain, Ontario, Erie, Huron & Michigan, &c. From the Year 1759 till this date, Excepting those employed at present upon Lake Champlain, Quebec, July 30, 1778, *WHC*, XI, 198-199. A Return of the Shipping on the Lakes Ontario, Erie and Huron, June 12, 1775, LeRoy, "Carleton as a Military Leader," pp. 624-625, however, reports only the *Haldimand* and *Charity* then in service on Lake Ontario, with two small sloops "on the stocks." It seems most likely, therefore, that *Caldwell* was begun at Navy Hall in 1774, launched during 1775 or perhaps even 1776, and named after Niagara's commandant. Caldwell's extant correspondence speaks only of tentative plans to build an unwieldy "scow" for use on the lower Niagara River; see Caldwell to Gage, Niagara, Aug. 14, Sept. 15, and Nov. 2, 1774, and Feb. 11, 1775, Gage Papers, Am. ser., vols. 122, 123, 124, and 126, WCL.

49. For commercial communications to and from Niagara, see: J[ames] E[llice] to Hayman Levy, Schenectady, Aug. 22, 1775, and J[ames] E[llice] to Alexander and William Macomb (at Detroit), Schenectady, Aug. 31, 1775, and J[ames] E[llice] to Pollard, Schenectady, Aug. 31, 1775, and R.

Ellice to Pollard, Schenectady, Dec. 23, 1775, and R. Ellice to John Stedman (at Niagara), Schenectady, Dec. 23, 1775, Phyn & Ellice LB, III, 216, 217, 217-218, 225-226, B&ECHS; R. Harvey Fleming, "Phyn, Ellice and Company of Schenectady," *University of Toronto: Contributions to Canadian Economics,* IV (1932), 33. For John Thompson's homestead and his role in the communications between Niagara and Johnson Hall, see: Daniel Claus to Haldimand, Montreal, Nov. 5, 1778, HP/BL Add. MSS. 21,774, fols. 1-13; Petition of John Thompson to Haldimand, Quebec, May 18, 1780, HP/BL Add. MSS. 21,874, fols. 163-164.

50. [Edmund] Armstrong to [Capt.] James Webb, Lisle Street, [London], Feb. 26, 1776, John Porteous Papers, Box 1 - Reel 1-A, Item 3, N-19, B&ECHS; Gen. Bigoe Armstrong to Sir James Caldwell, Bemers Street, [London], Aug. 3, 1776, B3/16/11, Caldwell Family Papers, Bagshawe Muniments, JRUL.

51. H[enry] H[amilton] to Sackville Hamilton, Niagara, Oct. 19, 1775, Joseph Redington and Richard A. Roberts, eds., *Calendar of Home Office Papers of the Reign of George III, 1760-1775, Preserved in the Public Record Office* (4 vols.; London: Her Majesty's Stationery Office, 1878-1899), IV, 449. Hamilton's appointment and journey to Detroit are related fully in Stevens, "His Majesty's 'Savage' Allies," pp. 364-366, 454, and 532-534. For the most reliable accounts of Hamilton's career, see: John D. Barnhart, ed., *Henry Hamilton and George Rogers Clark in the American Revolution, With the Unpublished Journal of Lieut. Govr. Henry Hamilton* (Crawfordsville, Ind.: R. E. Banta, 1951), pp. 1-103; Orville J. Jaebker, "Henry Hamilton: British Soldier and Colonial Governor" (Ph.D. dissertation, Indiana University, 1954); and Elizabeth Arthur, "Henry Hamilton," *DCB,* IV, 321-325.

52. This sketch of the Quebec Act is drawn from the fuller explanation given in Stevens, "His Majesty's 'Savage' Allies," pp. 256-259. See also: An act for making more effectual Provision for the Government of the Province of Quebec in North America, 1774, *DRCHC,* I, 401-415; Reginald Coupland, *The Quebec Act: A Study in Statesmanship* (Oxford: Clarendon Press, 1925); Hilda M. Neatby, *Quebec: The Revolutionary Age, 1760-1791* (Toronto: McClelland and Stewart Ltd., 1966), pp. 25-141; Jack M. Sosin, *Whitehall and the Wilderness: The Middle West in British Colonial Policy, 1760-1775* (Lincoln: University of Nebraska Press, 1961), pp. 240-249; Louise P. Kellogg, *The British Régime in Wisconsin and the Northwest* (Madison: The State Historical Society of Wisconsin, 1935), pp. 130-132; Russell, *British Régime,* pp. 73-74.

53. Edmund Burke to the Committee of Correspondence of the General Assembly of New York, [prob. London], Aug. 2, 1774, Edmund Burke, *The Correspondence of Edmund Burke,* ed. Thomas W. Copeland *et all.* (9 vols.; Cambridge: University Press: Chicago: University of Chicago Press, 1958-1970), III, 13-21.

54. Stevens, "His Majesty's 'Savage' Allies," pp. 362-367; and Stevens, "Indian Diplomacy of Capt. Lernoult", 77-78. The conflicts between lieutenant governors and garrison commanders appear frequently in the corrspondence of Detroit and Michilimackinac during the period 1775-1784. For one such incident involving a King's Regiment officer, see Paul L. Stevens, " 'Placing Proper Persons at Their Head': Henry Hamilton and the Establishment of Detroit's Revolutionary-Era Indian Department, 1777," *The Old Northwest,* XII (Summer, 1986). For a brief summary of the problems caused by having two senior officials at the various western posts, see: Lord George Germain to Haldimand, Whitehall, Mar. 17, 1980 (No. 23), HP/BL Add. MSS. 21,704, fol. 9; and Haldimand to Germain, Quebec, Oct. 25, 1780 (No. 50), HP/BL Add. MSS. 21,714, fol. 111.

55. Journal of Guy Johnson from May to November, 1775, and Guy Johnson to Germain, [London], Jan. 26, 1776, *NYCD,* VIII, 662, 657; Guy Johnson to Haldimand, Montreal, Sept. 9, 1782, HP/BL Add. MSS. 21,766, fols. 24-25; Guy Johnson to Haldimand, Montreal, Jan. 11, 1783, HP/BL Add. MSS, 21,768, fol. 128; [John Butler], Narrative of Lt. Col. Butler's Services in America, London, May, 1785, HP/BL Add. MSS. 21,875, fols. 191-192; *The Quebec Gazette,* Oct. 26, 1775; Cruikshank, *Butler's Rangers,* pp. 27-28. For Indian Department headquarters at Niagara, see: [Paul Long] to George Morgan, Pittsburgh, July 23, 1776, GMBL 1776, p. 43, PHMC; and John Dease to Sir John Johnson, Niagara, Aug. 21, 1784, Ernest A. Cruikshank, ed., *Records of Niagara, 1784-9* (Niagara-on-the-Lake, Ont.: Niagara Historical Society,]1929]), p. 46.

56. [Butler], Narrative of Lt. Col. Butler's Services in America, London, May, 1785, HP/BL Add. MSS. 21,875, fols. 191-192; Cruikshank, *Butler's Rangers,* pp. 27-28; Stevens, "His Majesty's 'Savage' Allies," pp. 519-52.

57. Regarding John Butler's background, see the works cited in n. 2 above and the additional references mentioned in Stevens, "His Majesty's 'Savage' Allies," pp. 1,869-1,870, no. 5, especially [John Butler], "Declaration of Colonel John Butler Received by Notary Beek, Montreal, Oct. 27, 1787," *Rapport de l'archiviste de la Province de Quebec pour 1924-1925* (Quebec: Ls-A. Proulx, 1925), pp. 393-396. His facility with the Seneca language can be discovered by carefully reading: Order of Guy Johnson, Guy Park, Oct. 6, 1774, *JP*, XIII, 684-685; Guy Johnson, Minutes of Indian Affairs 1774-1775, Nov. 8-11, 1774, RG 10, vol. 1829, 10-12, PAC; Hazel C. Mathews, *The Mark of Honour* (Toronto: University of Toronto Press, 1965), p. 36.

58. Pollard to Haldimand, Quebec, Oct. 20, 1781, HP/BL Add. MSS. 21,769, fols. 160-161; Proceedings of a Board assembled to examine and investigate all accounts and claims of Colonel Guy Johnson against Government, Quebec, Sept. 2-Oct. 24, 1783, HP/BL Add. MSS. 1,770, fols. 262; Daniel Claus, A General Detail of Col. Claus's Services since the Commencement of the War, 1755 to 1783, Claus Family Papers, XIV, 17-32, MG 19, Fl, PAC; Francis Goring to James Crespel, [Niagara, prob. Sept.,], 1779, "Goring Family Notes," pp. 24-27, W. H. Caniff Papers, Archives of Ontario, Toronto; James McGill to Isaac Todd, Montreal, Nov. 4 and 6, 1775, Redington and Roberts, eds., *Calendar of Home Office Papers,* IV, 483; Richard Butler to James Wilson, Fort Pitt, Apr. 8, 1776, *Am. Arch.,* 4-V, 816.
The nature of the "partnership" between Butler and Pollard and the documents relating to their relationship are examined in considerable detail in Stevens, "His Majesty's 'Savage' Allies,' pp. 521-524 and 2,040-2,043, n. 29. For a somewhat different but soundly-researched view, see Wilson, "Struggle for Wealth and Power at Fort Niagara," pp. 137-154.

59. Gen. Richard Montgomery to Gen. Philip Schuyler, Montreal, Nov. 19, 1775, *Am. Arch.,* 4-III, 1,682-1,683; R. Ellice to James Phyn, Schenectady, Dec. 3, 1775, and R. Ellice to Pollard and to John Stedman, Schenectady, Dec. 23, 1775, Phyn & Ellice LB, III, 223-224, 225-226, 226, B&ECHS; Stevens, "His Majesty's 'Savage' Allies," pp. 505-506, 528-529.

60. Hamilton to Carleton, Detroit, Dec. 4, 1775, Thwaites and Kellogg, eds., *Rev. on Upper Ohio,* pp. 127-135; Thomas Robison to Mr. Cornwell, Master of the Sloop *Chippawa,* Niagara, Dec. 7, 1775, and memorial of Adhemar St. Martin to Hamilton, Detroit, Aug. 10, 1776, and Caldwell to Carleton, Niagara, Aug. 19, 1776, HP/BL Add. MSS. 21,804, fols. 1, 2, 4 (St. Martin's memorial also in *MPHSC,* XIX, 319); Return of H.M.'s three vessels and five private vessels on Lakes Ontario, Erie and Huron, under command of Capt. Alxander Grant, Detroit, Aug. 2, 1776, *DAR,* X, #1918; James Bannerman to William Edgar, Detroit, May 20, 1777, William Edgar Papers, MG 19, A1, II, 615-616, PAC.

61. [Butler], Narrative of Lt. Col. Butler's Services in America, London, May, 1785, HP/BL Add. MSS. 21,785, fols. 191-192; [Butler], "Declaration of Colonel John Butler Received by Notary Beek, Montreal, Oct. 27, 1787, *Rapport de l'archiviste de la Province de Quebec pour 1924-1925,* pp. 395-396; Haldimand to Guy Johnson, Quebec, Jan. 3, 1781, HP/BL Add. MSS. 21,767, fols. 55-156; Gen. Allan Maclean to Haldimand, Niagara, Apr. 20, 1783, and Council with the Chiefs and Warrios of the Six Nations, Onondaga settlement of Tosioha, July 2, 1783, HP/BL Add. MSS. 21,763, fols. 38-39, 171-172; Schuyler to John Hancock, Albany, Jan. 31, and Feb. 13, 1776, PCC, Item 153, I, 490-492, 532-534 (also in *Am. Arch.,* 4-IV, 898, , 2); Cruikshank, *Butler's Rangers,* pp. 27-28; Graymont, *Iroquois in Revolution,* pp. 79-80; Stevens, "His Majesty's 'Savage' Allies," pp. 528-531.

62. Butler to Alexander McKee, Niagara, Feb. 29, 1776, *Am. Arch.,* 4-V, 818-819; James Dean to Schuyler, Oneida, Mar. 10, 1776, and Samuel Kirkland to Schuyler, Oneida, Mar. 12, 1776, PCC, Item 153, II, 79-82, 97-100 (also *Am. Arch.,* 4-V, 768-769, 772-773); Ebenezer Elmer, "Journal kept during an Expedition to Canada in 1776, by Ebenezer Elmer, Lieutenant in the Third Regiment of New Jersey Troops in the Continental Service, Commanded by Colonel Elias Dayton," *Proceedings of the New Jersey Historical Society,* 1st ser., II (1846-1847), 151 and 154 (entries at German Flats, July 17 and 20, 1776, reporting information from traders Peter and Richard Ryckman, recently escaped from Niagara); Mark E. Lender and James K. Martin, eds., *Citizen-Soldier: The Revolutionary War Journal of Joseph Bloomfield* (Newark: New Jersey Historical Society, 1982), p. 77 (entry at German Flats, July 18, 1776, reporting information from the Ryckmans); Guy Johnson, Minutes of Indian Affairs 1779-1780, Jan. 15, 1780, RG 10, vol. 1830, 113, PAC. The diplomacy between the British and the Six Nations during January-April, 1776, is narrated and documented more fully in Stevens, "His Majesty's 'Savage' Allies" pp. 576-581. See also Graymont, *Iroquois in Revolution,* pp. 86-93.

63. Schuyler to President of Congress, Albany, Feb. 15, 1776, and German Flats, July 17, 1776, PCC,

Item 153, I, 540-542, and II, 36-242 (also *Am. Arch.,* 4-IV, 1,156-1,157, and 5-I, 493-495); Kirkland to Timothy Edwards, Oneida, Apr. 6, 1776 (added to and transmitting James Dean to Kirkland, Kanghooragi, Mar. 22, 1776), Philip Schuyler Papers, box 13, NYPL (also in Penrose, comp., *Indian Affairs Papers,* pp. 38-39); Elmer, "Journal in 1776," II, 151 and 154 (information from the Ryckmans, German Flats, July 17 and 2, 1776); Lender and Martin, eds., *Citizen-Soldier: Bloomfield's Journal,* p. 77 (information from Ryckmans, German Flats, July 18, 1776).

64. John Butler to McKee, Niagara, Feb. 29, 1776, and Richard Butler to James Wilson, Fort Pitt, Apr. 8, 1776, *Am. Arch.,* 4-V, 818-819, 816; Journal of James Dean, Mar. 1-Apr. 3, 1776 *Am. Arch.,* 4-V, 1,102-1,103; Kirkland to Edwards, Oneida, Apr. 6, 1776, Schuyler Papers, box 13, NYPL; Meeting with Kayashuta and some Shawnese & Delawares, Fort Pitt, [July 6,] 1776, GMLB 1776, pp. 37-39, PHMC (also *Am. Arch.,* 5-I, 36, which gives the date); Stevens, "His Majesty's 'Savage' Allies, " pp. 577-578, 598.

65. Richard Butler to James Wilson, Fort Pitt, Mar. 18, 1776, Calrence M. Burton, ed., "Detroit during the Revolution," *MVHR,* II (June, 1915), 118-120; Information regarding Detroit [unsigned letter], Detroit, Apr. 2, 1776, Thwaites and Kellogg, eds., *Rev. on Upper Ohio,* pp. 147-151; John Neville to the President of the Committee of Safety, Fort Pitt, June 13, 1776, "Virginia Legislative Papers," *VMHB,* XVI (July, 1908), 53-55; Hamilton to Carleton, Detroit, June 16, 1776, Hamilton folder, Otto O. Fisher Papers, BHC, DPL; Elmer, "Journal in 1776," II, 151 and 154 (information from the Ryckmans, German Flats, July 17 and 20, 1776); Lender and Martin, eds., *Citizen-Soldier: Bloomfield's Journal,* p. 77 (information from the Ryckmans, German Flats, July 18, 1776); George Morgan, Intelligence from Detroit by a Mr. Heron, [Pitsburgh], July 27, 1776, GMLB 1776, pp. 49-50, PHMC; Commissioners for the Middle Department to Hancock, Pittsburgh, Aug. 16, 1776, GMLB, II, CLP; Hamilton to Earl of Dartmouth, Detroit, Aug. 29-Sept. 2, 1776, CO 42/35, fols. 190-197, PRO (also *MPHSC,* X, 264-270); Jehu Hay to John Butler, Vincennes, Jan. 28, 1779, HP/BL Add. MSS. 21,782, fols. 183-184. The reference here to the withdrawal of Captain Lord's command from Kaskaskia to Detroit is drawn from the much more detailed and extensively docmented account in Stevens, "His Majesty's 'Savage' Allies," pp. 459-465, 490-494, 670-676,

66. The details of the Onondaga council are in Journal of James Dean, Mar. 1-Apr. 3, 1776, *Am. Arch.,* 4-V, 1,100-1,104. References to Chippewas and Ottawas at Niagara in May-June, 1776, are found in: Oneida Chiefs to Schuyler, Oneida, May 22, 1776 (written by Kirkland), *NYCD,* VIII, 688-689; Kirkland to Schuyler, Lake George, June 8, 1776, PCC, Item 153, II, 202-204 (also *Am. Arch.,* 4-VI, 764); [Long] to Morgan, Pittsburgh, July 23, 1776, and Speech of Keyasheeta to Morgan, Pittsburgh, July 24, 1776, GMLB 1776, pp. 43-49, 36-37, PHMC: Speech of the White Mingo to the Commissioners of the Middle Department, Pittsburgh, Aug. 21, 1776, and Speech of the Commissioners to the Chippewas, Pittsburgh, Sept. 25, 1776, GMLB, II, CLP. See also: Graymont, *Iroquois in Revolution,* pp. 90-91; Ralph T. Pastore, "The Board of Commissioners for Indian Affairs in the Northern Department and the Iroquois Indians, 1775-1778" (Ph.D. dissertation, University of Notre Dame, 1972), pp. 20-122; Stevens, "His Majesty's 'Savage' Allies" pp. 583-587, 663-664, and 2,064-2,065, nn. 28 and 29.

67. The story behind the mission of Goddard, Lorimier, and Walker to Oswegatchie and Niagara must be extracted from fragments of circumstantial evidence. It is told and documented fully in Stevens, "His Majesty's 'Savage' Allies," pp. 567-576.

68. Jean-Baptiste Badeaux, "Invasion du Canada par les Américains en 1775" (journal entries for Apr. 24 and 27, and May 13, 1776), Hospice Anthelme J. B. Verreau, *Invasion du Canada, collection de mémoires recrueillis et annotés par M. l'abbé Verreau, prêtre* (Montréal: Société historique de Montréal, 1873), pp. 203, 205, 212; John F. Roche, ed., "Quebec Under Siege, 1775-1776; The 'Memorandums' of Jacob Danford," *CHR,* L (Mar., 1969), 83 (entry for Apr. 23, 1776); Sheldon S. Cohen, ed., *Canada Preserved: The Journal of Captain Thomas Ainslie* (New York: New York University Press, 1969), pp. 80, 82-83 (entries for Apr. 20 and 23, 1776); W. T. P. Short, ed., "Journal of the Principal Occurences during the Siege of Quebec by the American Revolutionists under Generals Montgomery and Arnold in 1775-76 [Attributed to Sir John Hamilton]" (London: Simpkin and Co., 1824), rpt. pp. 55-101, vol. II, *Blockade of Quebec in 1775-1776 by the American Revolutionists (Les Bastonnais),* ed. Fred C. Wurtele, Lit. and Hist. Soc. of Quebec, Seventh and Eighth Series of Historical Documents (2 vols.; Quebec: Literary and Historical Society of Quebec, 1905-1906), II, 96 (entry for Apr. 20, 1776); Gen. Bigoe Armstrong to Sir James Caldwell, Bemers Street, [London], Aug. 3, 1776, B3/16/11, Caldwell Family Papers, Bagshawe Muniments, JRUL; Gen. David Wooster to Schuyler, Montreal, Mar. 5, 1776, PCC, Item 153, II, 61-63 (*Am. Arch.,* 4-V, 416-417); Moses Hazen to Edward Antill,

Montreal, Apr. 20, 1776, HP/BL Add. MSS. 21,687, fols. 261-262.

69. Simon McTavish to William Edgar, Michilimackinac, May 12, and June 9, 1776, and James Bannerman to Edgar, Michilimackinac, June 10 and 23, 1776, William S. Wallace, ed., *Documents Relating to the North West Company* (Toronto: The Champlain Society, 1934), pp. 48-53; De Peyster, *Miscellanies,* pp. 2-3; [De Pyester] to Louis Joseph Ainsse, Orders, Michilimackinac, June 17, 1776, Joseph Louis Ainasse Papers, 1763-1874, MG 23, G3, XXVI, #56, PAC; De Peyster to Charles de Langlade, Michilimackinac, July 4, 1776, *WHC,* XVIII, 355-356; Rhymed chronicle of De Peyster's speech at L'Arbre Croche, July 4, 1779, De Peyster, *Miscellanies,* pp. 5-15; Armour and Widder, *At the Crossroads,* pp. 52-55; Stevens, "His Majesty's 'Savage' Allies" pp. 587-588, 612-613.

70. No single source explains more than a small part of the story of Butler's recruitment of this "war party." Caldwell's words are reported in: Oneida Chiefs to Scuyler, Oneida, May 22, 1776 (written by Kirkland), *NYCD,* VIII, 688-690. To understand the episode completely, consult also: [Butler], Narrative of Lt. Col. Butler's Services in America, London, May, 1785, HP/BL Add. MSS. 1,875, fols. 191-192; McTavish to Edgar, Michilimackinac, June 9, 1776, Wallace, ed., *Docs. Rel. to N.W. Co.,* pp. 49-50; [Long] to Morgan, Pittsburgh, July 24, 1776, and Simon Girty's report to Morgan, Pittsburgh, July 23, 1776, and Speech of Keyasheeta to Morgan, Pittsburgh, July 26, 1776, GMBL 1776, pp. 36-37, 49, 53-54, PHMC; Speech of the White Mingo to the Commissioners of the Middle Department, Pittsburgh, Aug. 21, 776, and Speech of the Commissioners to the Chippewas, Pittsburgh, Sept. 25, 1776, GMLB, II, CLP; Schuyler to Washington, Fort George, May 31, 1776, *Am. Arch.,* 4-V, 640; Elmer, "Journal in 1776," II, 151 and 154 (information from the Ryckmans, German Flats, July 17 and 2, 1776); Lender and Martin, eds., *Citizen-Soldier: Bloomfield's Journal,* p. 77 (information from the Ryckmans, German Flats, July 18, 1776); Guy Johnson, Minutes of Indian Affairs 1779-1780, Jan. 28, 1780, RG 10, vol. 1830, 130, PAC; [Guy Johnson], Review of Col. Johnson's transactions, Montreal, Mar. 24, 1782, HP/BL Add. MSS. 21,766, fols. 29-31; Chevalier [Claude-Nicholas-Guillaume] de Lorimier, "Mes services pendant la guerre américaine de 1775," Verreau, ed., *Invasion du Canada,* pp. 270, 274; John Norton, *The Journal of Major John Norton,* 1816, ed. Carl F. Klinck and James J. Talman (Toronto: The Champlain Society, 1970), p. 272. Especially useful are the Six Nations' explanations of this affair to the rebels; see the speeches of the Onondaga sachem Onwasqwinghte and the Cayuga chief Ojageghte (Fish-Carrier) in Gen. Schuyler's Conference with the Indians of the Six Nations, German Flats, Aug. 8-13, 1776, *Am. Arch.,* 5-I, 1,046-1,048. See also: Graymont, *Iroquois in Revolution,* pp. 95-97; Stevens, "His Majesty's 'Savage' Allies," pp. 587-591.

71. The two detailed accounts of Forster's expedition by its British participants are: Capt. Andrew Parke, J[acob] Maurer, and Hugh MacKay, "Account of the Events at the Cedars, Montreal, September 6, 1776 (certified correct by Capt. George Forster, Montreal, Sept. 27, 1776)," published as part of *An Authentic Narrative of Facts Relating to the Exchange of Prisoners taken at the Cedars …* (London, 1777); and Lorimier, "Mes services pendant la guerre américaine de 1774," Verreau, ed., *Invasion du Canada,* pp. 268-283 (app., pp. 19-31 also contains Capt. Parke's "Account," though in French translation). The sketch given here, however, is based on the detailed narrative of Forster's campaign given in Stevens, "His Majesty's 'Savage' Allies," pp. 615-631. See also: Stanley, *Canada Invaded,* pp. 117-123; Robert M. Hatch, *Thrust for Canada: The American Attempt on Quebec in 1775-1776* (Boston: Houghton Miflin Co., 1979), pp. 196-208; Graymont, *Iroquois in Revolution,* p. 94.

72. This overview of Sir John Johnson's activities summarizes the more extensive account in Stevens, "His Majesty's 'Savage' Allies," pp. 580-583, 591-596, 640-641, 657-658. See also: Graymont, *Iroquois in Revoltion,* pp. 81-85, 92-94; Mabel G. Walker, "Sir John Johnson, Loyalist," *MVHR,* III (Dec., 1916), 325-330; Pastore, "The Board of Commissioners and the Iroquois," pp. 98-111; Fryer, *King's Men,* pp. 69-72. The specific references to the contacts between Niagara and Johnson Hall, New York City, and Boston during this period are: Gen. William Howe to Dartmouth, Boston, Jan. 16, 1776, and to William Tryon and to Officer Commanding at Niagara, Boston, Jan. 11, 1776, *DAR,* X, 189, #820 and #820vi-vii (letter to Datmouth also in *Am. Arch.,* 4-IV, 699-702); Tryon to Dartmouth, Ship *Dutchess of Gordon* off New York, Feb. 8, 1776, *NYCD,* VIII, 663-664; I.G.R.A. to Tryon, New York, Apr. 27, 1776, *DAR,* X, 280, #1437xxxviii; Dean to Schuyler, Oneida, Mar. 10, 1776, and Kirkland to Schuyler, Oneida, Mar. 12, 1776, PCC, Item. 153, II, 79-82, 97-100; Col. Elias Dayton to Schuyler, Johnstown, May 22 and 24, 1776, PCC, Item 153, II, 157-159, 169-170 (also *Am. Arch.,* 4-VI, 644-645, 646-647); Lender and Martin, eds., *Citizen-Soldier: Bloomfield's Journal,* pp. 52-54 (entry at Johnstown, May 22, 1776); Schuyler to Washington, Albany, June 19, 1776, PCC, Item 153, II, 219-223 (also *Am. Arch.,* 4-VI, 974-975); Declaration of Thomas Gumersall, Staten Island, Aug. 6, 1776, *NYCD,* VIII, 683; Remarks of Capt. John Deserontyon's Services to the King of Great Britain &c., Niagara, 1809, Draper MSS., 14F49-49(5);

Robert W. Venables, "Tryon County, 1775-1783: A Frontier in Revoltion" (Ph.D. dissertation, Vanderbilt University, 1967), p. 124.

73. Although neither Caldwell nor Butler — nor, in fact, any British source — left any mention of this council at Niagara, detailed accounts are provided by George Morgan's spy, Paul Long, by Kayashuta, and by Albany trader Peter Ryckman (who escaped from Niagara on June 27, 1776). See: [Long] to Morgan, Pittsburgh, July 23, 1776, and Meeting with Kayahuta and some Shawnese & Delawares, Fort Pitt, [July 6,] 1776, and Speech of Keyasheeta to Morgan, Pittsburgh, July 24, 1776, GMLB 1776, pp. 43-49, 37-39, 36-37, PHMC; Schuyler to Hancock, German Flats, July 17, 1776, PCC, Item 153, II, 236-243. For a more complete account of the council and its source documents, see: Stevens, "His Majesty's 'Savage' Allies," pp. 658-665 and 2,093-2,095, n. 34. See also Gramont, Iroquois in Revolution, pp. 97-100.

74. For the details of this Onondaga council, see: Girty's report to Morgan, Pittsburgh, July 26, 1776, and Meeting with Kayashuta and some Shawnese & Delawares, Fort Pitt, [July 6,] 1776, and Speech of Keyasheeta to Morgan, Pittsburgh, July 24, 1776, GMLB 1776, pp. 52-58, 37-39, 36-37, PHMC; speech of the White Mingo to the Commissioners, Pittsburgh, Aug. 1, 1776, GMLB, II, CLP; Graymont, Iroquois in Revolution, pp. 102-103; Stevens, "His Majesty's 'Savage' Allies," pp. 665-670 and 2,095, n. 35.

75. Pollard to Bolton, Niagara, June 2, 1778, and Bolton to Carleton, Niagara, June 5, 1778, HP/BL Add. MSS. 1,760, fols. 24, 22-3; A List of Houses, Store-Houses, &c. at Niagara, belonging to Messrs. Taylor and Forsyth, which have not the Commanding Officers permission (in writing) agreeable to a Form received from Canada in 1779, HP/BL Add. MSS. 1,760, fol. 266; Account of all the Merchandize &ca Debits & other Property belonging to the Copartnership of Taylor & Duffin, Niagara, May 27, 1779, together with an incomplete letter, William Talor to William Duffin, Niagara, n.d. [1779], William Duffin, "Account of Merchandise of Taylor & Duffin, Niagara, 1779," MG 23, H II, 2, PAC: Francis Goring to James Crespel, [Niagara, prob. Sept.,] 1779, "Goring Family Notes," pp. 24-27, W. H. Canniff Papers, Archives of Ontario, Toronto.

76. Dartmouth to Gage, Whitehall, Aug. 2, 1776, Gage Corr., II, 204-206; Carleton to Caldwell and to Lord, Montreal, July 19, 1776, HP/BL Add. MSS. 21,699, pp. 19, 21; Hamilton to [Carleton], Detroit, Sept. 4, 1776, Hamilton folder, Otto O. Fisher Papers, BHC, DPL; Carleton to Germain, Chambly, Sept. 28, 1776, CO 42/35, fols. 171-177, PRO; Memorial of Capt. Hugh Lord to the Commissioners for Trade and Plantations, [Dec. 3, 1776], DAR, X, 417, #2396; Morgan, Intelligence from Detroit received at Pittsburgh, Dec. 12, 1776, Michigan Collection, WCL.

77. Tryon County Committee to N.Y. Congress, Tryon County, Feb. 17, 1776, Am. Arch., 4-IV, 1,180-1,181; Schuyler to Hancock, Fort George, May 3, 1776, and Dayton to Schuyler (encl. two depositions), Johnstown, May 24, 1776, and Schuyler to Committee of Albany, Fort George, May 27, 1776, Am. Arch., 4-V, 1,181-1,182, and 4-VI, 646, 648-649; Col. Frederick Bellinger to Col. Frederick Vischer, German Flats, June 7, 1776, and Schuyler to Hancock, Fort George, June 8, 1776, and Kirkland to Schuyler, Lake George, June 8, 1776, and Schuyler to Washington, Albany, June 10, 11, and 19, 1776, Am. Arch., 4-VI, 762, 762-763, 764, 795-796, 819-820, 974-975; Elmer, "Journal in 1776," II, 123-125, 132 (entries for June 6-10, 28, 1776); Lender and Martin, eds., Citizen-Soldier: Bloomfield's Journal, pp. 60-93 (entries for June 6-July 31, 1776); Commissioners for the Middle Department to Committee of Congress for Indian Affairs, Pittsburgh, July 3, 1776, GMLB, II, CLP; Speech of the Cayuga chief Ojageghte (Fish-Carrier) in Gen. Schuyler's Conference with the Indians of the Six Nations, German Flats Aug. 8-13, 1776, Am. Arch., 5-I, 1,047-1,048; Hamilton to Dartmouth, Detroit, Aug. 29-Sept. 2, 1776, CO 42/35, fols. 190-197, PRO; John Dusler, Declaration in order to obtain the benefit of the Acts of Congress passed June 7, 1832, Herkimer County, N.Y., Feb. 12, 1833, Draper MSS., 3F35-36; Pastore, "The Board of Commissioners and the Iroquois," pp. 127-129; Stevens, "His Majesty's 'Savage' Allies," pp. 654-656, 695-687.

78. Schuyler to President of Congress, German Flats, July 17, 1776, PC, Item 153, II, 236-242; Elmer, "Journal in 1776," II, 151 and 154 (entries for July 17 and 20, 1776); Lender and Martin, eds., Citizen-Soldier: Bloomfield's Journal, pp. 76-77 (entry for July 18, 1776); [Long] to Morgan, Pittsburgh, July 23, 1776, and Girty's report to Morgan, Pittsburgh, July 26, 1776, GMLB 1776, pp. 43-49, 52-58, PHMC; Advices from the Indians by George Morgan, Philadelphia, Aug. 15, 1776, Am. Arch., 5-I, 137-138; Speech of the White Mingo to the Commissioners, Pittsburgh, Aug. 21, 1776, GMLB, II, CLP; Speech of the Onondaga sachem Onwasqwinghte in Gen. Schuyler's Conference with the Indians of the Six

Nations, German Flats Aug. 8-13, 1776, *Am. Arch.*, 5-I, 1,046,1,047.

79. Desite a long, adventurous, and well documented career in the British service in the west, William Caldwell (1746 or 1747-Feb. 20, 1822) still lacks, at this writing, the scholarly biography he deserves. Therefore, for biographical background, see: Return of the Officers of the Corps of Rangers commanded by Lt. Col. John Butler, n.d., HP/BL Add. MSS. 21,827, fol. 348; Recollections of Capt. Wm. Caldwell, son of Capt. William Caldwell of Butler's Rangers, Draper MSS, 17S213-214, 229-230; Recollections of James Caldwell (born 1785), son of Capt. William Caldwell of Butler's Rangers, Draper MSS., 17S235-237; Ernest J. Lajeunesse, ed., *The Windsor Border Region: Canada's Southernmost Frontier: A Collection of Documents* (Toronto: The Champlain Society, 1960), p. 114, n. 23; Askin, *Askin Papers,* ed. Quaife, I, 243-244, n. 39 (which cites other sources pertaining to Caldwell's career). Some additional information, based on an 1915 autobiographical memorial (now in the Archives of Ontario), can be found in a study of his half-Mohawk son: James A. Clifton, "Merchant, Soldier, Broker, Chief: A Corrected Obituary of Captain Billy Caldwell," *Journal of the Illinois State Historical Society,* LXXI (Aug., 1978), 186-187, 192. For his appointment in the Indian Department, see: A List of Colonel Johnsons Department of Indian Affairs, [prob. Niagara, 1777], WO 28/10, fol. 402, PRO; A List of Officers employed in the Indian department with their rank and pay (encl. in John Butler to Carleton, Niagara, June 15, 1777), CO 42/36, fols. 321-322, PRO. The escape of William Caldwell and four captured British officers (Richardson, Hume, Cubbage, and one other) in June-July, 1776, is revealed in: The Examination of William Poor ..., In Commitee, Lancaster, July 26, 1776, and The Examination of John White..., [In Committee, Lancaster, July 26, 1776], *Am. Arch.*, 5-I, 596-597, 597-599; John Harris to Owen Biddle, Paxton, July 29, 1776, *Pennsylvania Archives ...*, ed. Samuel Hazard *et al.* (138 vols. in 9 ser.; Philadelphia and Harrisburg, 1852-1935), ser. 1, IV, 789-790; Officials of Westmoreland to the Connecticut Delagates in the Continental Congress, Westmoreland, Aug. 6, 1776, Julian P. Boyd and Robert J. Taylor, eds., *The Susquehannah Company Papers* (11 vols.; Ithaca, N.Y.: Cornell University Press, for the Wyoming Historical and Geological Society, Wilkes-Barre, Pa., 1930-1971), VII, 18-20.

80. Walter Butler's whereabouts during February-September, 1776, remain to be discovered by some diligent researcher. His activities during June, 1775-February, 1776, are touched upon in Stevens, "His Majesty's 'Savage' Allies," pp. 328-340, 385-406, 418-454, 494-504, 548-555, but see specifically: Lyman C. Draper's notes from Guy Johnson's Account, Mar. 25-Sept. 24, 1775 (copied from William Johnson MSS. papers, vol. XXVI, no. 82 [since destroyed by fire]), Draper MSS., 15F86; Account of the Skirmish on the 25th September, by Nauticus *The Quebec Gazette,* Oct. 19, 1775; [Edmund] Armstrong to [Capt.] James Webb, Lisle Street, [London], Feb. 26, 1776, John Porteous Papers, Box 1- Reel 1-A, Item 3, N-19, B&ECHS; A speech delivered by the Hurons, ..., being in Council in presence of Lieut. Colo. John Caldwell, Niagara, Sept. 18, 1776, Military Papers of Gen. Peter Gansevoort, vol. II, Gansevoort-Lansing Collection, NYPL; Ens. Walter Butler to Charles de Langlade at Little Niagara, Fort Erie, Nov. 16, 1776, *WHC,* XVIII, 356; Guy Johnson to Haldimand, Montreal, Jan. 11, 1783, HP/BL Add. MSS. 21,768, fol. 128; John Long, *Voyages and Travels in the Years 1768-1788,* ed. Milo M. Quaife (1791; repub. Chicago: R. R. Donnelley & Sons Co., 1922), p. 26; [Cannon], *Historical Record of the King's, Liverpool Regiment* (1883 ed.), p. 239; Charters, "Walter Butler," *DCB,* IV, 121-122; Neil B. Renolds, "The Butlers of Wyoming and Cherry Valley," *The American Genealogist,* XXXVI (Oct., 1960), 201-203; Cruikshank, *Butler's Rangers,* pp. 24-28; Graymont, *Iroquois in Revolution,* pp. 79, 81; Kelsay, *Joseph Brant,* pp. 149, 159. Both the usually reliable Cruikshank, "Memoir of Captain Walter Butler," pp. 284-285, and the often unreliable Swiggett, *War Out of Niagara,* pp. 64-72, overlook Walter Butler's trip to England and mistakenly presume that he accompanied his father to Niagara in November, 1775. Swiggett, *op. cit.,* pp. 71-72 also states that Ens. Walter Butler was present at the British victory over rebel forces at the Cedars near Montreal on May 19-20, 1776, but a thorough search through all the extant contemporary sources, including the report written by the 8th Regiment officers involved, shows that young Butler did not take part in that campaign; see Stevens, *op. cit.,* pp. 615-631 and 2,074-2,981, nn. 1-11.

81. Carleton to Foster, Montreal, June 20, 1776, and Carleton to Caldwell, Montreal, July 19, 1776, HP/BL Add. MSS. 21,699, pp. 9, 19; Information from Lt. Col. Allan Maclean (departed Quebec, July 27, 1776), 263; Gen. John Burgoyne to Gen. Henry Clinton, Quebec, Nov. 7, 1776, Henry Clinton Papers, WCL; [William Knox], Precis of operations on Canadian frontier ... (incl. notes on a "Conversation with General Burgoyne after his arrival in England," [Dec., 1776]), CO 5/253, fols. 46-54, PRO; Gerald Howson, *Burgoyne of Saratoga: A Biography (New York: Times Books, 1979), p. 119; Richard J. Hargrove, Jr., General John Burgoyne* (Newark: University of Delaware Press, 1983), p. 99, no. 76; Gerald S. Brown, *The American Secretary: The Colonial Policy of Lord George Germain,*

1775-1778 (Ann Arbor: University of Michigan Press, 1963), pp. 88-89.

82. Carleton to Caldwell, to De Peyster, to Hamilton, and to Foster, Montreal, July 19, 1776, HP/BL Add. MSS. 21,699, pp. 19-20. A complete account of the recruitment of the Michilimackinac Indians and their activities in Montreal is given in Stevens, "His Majesty's 'Savage' Allies," pp. 611-613, 679-683, 694-71. See also: Armour and Widder, *At the Crossroads,* pp. 52-56; Kellogg, *British Régime,* pp. 35-136; and Paul L. Stevens, "A Minnesota Dakota Chief in Quebec City, 1776: New Information Regarding Wabasha's Visit to the Governor of British Canada," to appear in a 1987 or 1988 issue of *Minnesota History.*

83. No specific record of Hay's visit to Niagara seems to exist, but he must have stopped there in mid or late August because he departed Detroit after August 5 and reached Montreal before September 9, 1776. See: Hamilton to [Carleton], Detroit, 1776 (without date, delivered by Jehu Hay), [Calendar and précis of letters from Henry Hamilton, Jan. 24, 1776-July 3, 1777], HP/BL Add. MSS. 21,841, fols. 57-50; Macomb Journal No. 2, p. 88 (entry at Detroit, Aug 5 1776), Alexander and William Macomb Papers, BHC, DPL; Carleton to Hamilton, Chambly, Sept. 9, 1776, HP/BL Add. MSS. 21,699, p. 35 (also *MPHSC,* X, 264); Isaac Todd to William Edgar, Montreal, Sept. 12, 1776, William Edgar Papers, MG 19, A1, 11, pp. 541-542, PAC.

84. Interestingly, the three sources (two similar copies existing for one of the documents) that give information about this council record only the viewpoints of its Indian participants. See: A speech delivered by the Hurons ... being in Council in presence of Lieut. Colo. John Caldwell, Niagara, Sept. 18, 1776, Military Papers of Gen. Peter Gansevoort, vol. II, Gansevoort-Lansing Collection, NYPL (paraphrased and summarized in Stone, *Life of Brant,* II, 3-4, n. †); Intelligence from an [Seneca] Indian To Be Kept Private, [Pittsburgh], Sept. 3, 1776, Jasper Yeates Correspondence 1762-1780, The Historical Society of Pennsylvania, Philadelphia; Intelligence from an [Seneca] Indian, [Pitsburgh, Sept., 1776], GMLB, II, CLP; Aaron Kanonaron (Hill) to his brother David, residing at the lower Mohawk village, Niagara, Oct. 28, 1776 (intercepted; translated by Kirkland, Nov. 11, 1776), PCC, Item 153, II, 497-499 (also *Am. Arch.,* 5-III, 770-771). For secondary accounts of this council, see: Graymont, *Iroquois in Revolution,* p. 106; Wallace, *Death and Rebirth of the Seneca,* pp. 131-134; and Stevens, "His Majesty's 'Savage' Allies," pp. 773-781. For the details of the German Flats council, see: Graymont, *op. cit.,* pp. 106-108; Stevens, *op. cit.,* pp. 715-724; Pastore, "The Board of Commissioners and the Iroquois," pp. 135-158.

85. A complete account of Hamilton's council and the formation of the intertribal coalition is given in Stevens, "His Majesty's 'Savage' Allies," pp.760-774. For Caldwell's request for Indians from Detroit, see: Hamilton to [Carleton], Detroit, Sept. 4, 1776, Hamilton folder, Otto O. Fisher Papers, BHC, DPL.

86. In order to reconstruct the discussions and decisions of this Niagara council, it is necessary to examine the sources cited in n. 84 and also: Samuel Kirkland, *The Journals of Samuel Kirkland: 18th-century Missionary to the Iroquois, Government Agent, Father of Hamilton College,* ed. Walter Pilkington (Clinton, N.Y.: Hamilton College, 1980), pp. 112-113 (entries for Oct. 9 and 25, 1776); William Johnston to ?, Unadilla, Sept. 18, 1776, New York (State), Legislature, *Journals of the Provincial Congress, Provincial Convention, Committee of Safety and Council of Safety of the State of New-York, 1775-1776-1777* (2 vols.: Albany: Thurlow Weed, 1842), II, 19; Speech of Ojistarale (The Grasshopper), an Oneida chief, to Col. Samuel Elmore, Commandant of Fort Schuyler [Stanwix], Nov. 18, 1776, *Am. Arch.,* 5-III, 754-755; Carl J. Fliegel, comp., *Index to the Records of the Moravian Mission among the Indians of North America* (New Haven, Conn.: Research Publications, Inc., 1970), pp. 1,040 ("Senecas": 9-14-1776) and 1,049 ("Six Nations": 9-19-1776, and 11-12/20/24-1776); Speech by the Wyandot chief Tseendattong on June 17, 1777, in Proceedings of a council held at Detroit, by Lt. Gov. Hamilton, June 17-24, 1777, CO 42/37, fols. 70-77, PRO; Meeting of the Commissioners for Indian Affairs in the Northern Department with Deputies from the Onondaga Nation, Albany, Aug. 15, 1778, PCC, Item 166, pp. 387-394; Speech of the Six Nations to the Hurons [Wyandots], Niagara, Feb. 13, 1779, HP/BL Add. MSS. 21,779, fols. 21-22; [Butler], Narrative of Lt. Col. Butler's Services in America, London, May, 1785, HP/BL Add. MSS. 21,875, fols. 191-192.

87. For the content and destinations of the messages dispatched from this council, see the speech of the Hurons *et al.* and the letter of Aaron Kanonaron cited in n. 84, and also: [Butler], Narrative of Lt. Col. Butler's Services in America, London, May, 1785, HP/BL Add. MSS. 21,875, fols. 191-192; Kirkland, *Journals,* pp. 112-113; Fliegel, comp., *Moravian Records Index,* p. 1,049 ("Six Nations": 11-

12/20/24-1776); David Zeisberger to Morgan, Coshocton, Nov. 21, 1776, GMLB, I, CLP; Guy Johnson to Germain, New York, Nov. 25, 1776, *NYCD,* VIII, 688; De Peyster to Carleton, Michilimackinac, Feb. 18, 1777, CO 42/36, fol. 132, PRO (also *MPHSC,* X, 271); Speech by Tseendattong on June 17, 1777, in Council held at Detroit, June 17-24, 1777, CO 42/37, fols. 70-77, PRO.

88. [Butler], Narrative of Lt. Col. Butler's Service in America, London, May, 1785, HP/BL Add. MSS. 21,875, fols. 191-192; Kirkland, *Journals,* p. 112 (entry for Oct. 9, 1776); Aaron Kanonaron (Hill) to his brother David, Niagara, Oct. 28, 1776, PCC, Item. 53, II, 497-499; Speech of Ojistarale to Elmore, Nov. 18, 1776, *Am. Arch.,* 5-III, 754-755.

89. Carleton to Caldwell, off Pointe au Fer, Oct. 6, 1776, and Crown Point, Oct. 29, 1776, HP/BL Add. MSS. 21,699, pp. 49, 59; Capt. Edward Foy to Caldwell, Quebec, Oct. 30, 1776 (circular letter), HP/BL Add. MSS. 21,678, fol. 190. See also: Carleton to Hamilton and to De Peyster, off Pointe au Fer, Oct. 6, 1776, HP/BL Add. MSS. 21,699, p. 49; Ens. Walter Butler to Charles de Langlade at Little Niagara, Fort Erie, Nov. 6, 1776, WHC, XVIII, 356.

90. Ens. John Caldwell to Sir James and Lady Elizabeth Caldwell (his parents), Detroit, Mar. 31, 1777, B3/13/111, Caldwell Family Papers, Bagshawe Muniments, JRUL; Ens. Durell Saumarez to Thomas Saumarez, Niagara, Apr. 10, 1777, Durell Saumarez Papers, MG 23, K10, I, 1-4, PAC; Eulogy for Lt. Col. John Caldwell, *The Quebec Gazette,* May 1, 1777. See also: John Caldwell to Lady Caldwell (his mother), Bromley, Dec. 26,1770, B3/29/108, and Lt. Col. J[ohn] C[aldwell] to Sir James Caldwell, Bath, Jan. 7, 1773, B3/13/86, and Lt. John Caldwell, Memorial to Lord Jeffery Amherst, Exeter, 20th [no month given] 1781, B3/38/4, Caldwell Family Papers, *loc. cit.;* Oneida Chiefs to Schuyler, Oneida, May 22, 1776 written by Kirkland), *NYCD,* VIII, 688-690; Haldimand to Germain, Quebec, Jan. 28, 1780 (private), HP/BL Add. MSS. 1,714, fol. 89.

91. Lernoult had become the regiment's second-ranking captain and its second-senior officer in America after elderly Capt. James Webb (whose name was struck from the regimental roll as of November 22, 1775) either died at Niagara during the winter of 1775-1776 or retired to England during the summer of 1776. See: Summary of a letter from Hamilton to Carleton Detroit, Nov. 13, 1776, [Calendar and précis of letters from Henry Hamilton, Jan. 24, 1776-July 3, 1777], HP/BL Add. MSS. 21,841, fols. 57-59; Adjutant General's Orderly Book of the British Army in Canada, May 8, 1776-1784, Quebec, Jan. 31, 1777, p. 35, MS/Great Britain—Army in America, WCL; Carleton to Lernoult, Commanding at Niagara, Quebec, Feb. 2, 1777, HP/BL Add. MSS. 1,678, fol. 191; [Cannon], *Historical Record of the King's, Liverpool Regiment* (1883 ed.), p. 215.

SELECT BIBLIOGRAPHY

This bibliography lists all materials mentioned in the notes and also a number of other works that the author found useful but did not cite specifically.

I. **Primary Sources**
   A. Manuscript Collections
Archives of Ontario, Toronto, Ontario
    W. H. Canniff Papers, "Goring Family Notes"
British Library, London, England
    Sir Frederick Haldimand Papers, Additional Manuscripts 21,661-21,892 (microfilm copies in Public Archives of Canada, Ottawa; The Newberry Library, Chicago; and the author's personal collection)
Buffalo and Erie County Historical Society, Buffalo, New York
    Letter books of Phyn and Ellice (merchants at Schenectady, New York, 1767-1776 (3 volumes)
    Papers of John Porteous (fur trader and merchant at Detroit and Michilimackinac to October, 1776; loyalist, merchant in New York City), 1765-1857
Burton Historical Collection, Detroit Public Library, Detroit Michigan
    William Edgar Papers
    Otto O. Fisher Papers
    Henry Hamilton Papers
    William Kirby Papers
    Alexander and William Macomb Papers
Carnegie Library of Pittsburgh, Pittsburgh, Pennsylvania
    George Morgan, Letterbooks I-III, 1775-1779 (microfilm copy)
Ewart Public Library, Dumfries, Scotland
    Collection of Papers Relating to Col. A. S. de Peyster
The Historical Society of Pennsylvania, Philadelphia, Pennsylvania
    Jasper Yeates Papers, Correspondence 1762-80
King's Regiment Collection, Merseyside County Museums, Liverpool, England
    Indian souvenirs belonging to Colonel Arent S. De Peyster
National Archives and Records Service, Washington, D.C.
    Papers of the Continental Congress, 1774-1789 (M247), Records of the Continental Congress and the Constitutional Convention, Record Group 360 (microfilm copy)
        Item 153, Letters from Major General Philip Schuyler, June, 1775-June 1785
        Item 166, Letters and Papers Relating to Canadian Affairs, Sullivan's Expedition, and the Northern Indians, 1775-1779
New York Public Library, New York City, New York
    Military papers of Gen. Peter Gansevoort, Gansevoort-Lansing Collection
    Philip Schuyler Papers, boxes 13 and 14
Pennsylvania Historical and Museum Commission, Harrisburg, Pennsylvania
    George Morgan Letterbook for 1776 (typescript copy)
Public Archives of Canada, Ottawa, Ontario
    Joseph Louis Ainsse Papers, 1763-1874 (MG 23, G III, 26)
    Claus Family Papers, 1755-1856 (MG 19, F1)
    Colonel Office Papers (CO) 42 (MG 11 — microfilm from Public Record Office, London)
    William Duffin, "Account of Merchandise of Taylor & Duffin, Niagara, 1779" (MG 23, H II, 2)
    William Edgar Papers (MG 19, Al, 11 — photocopies)
    Francis Goring Papers, 1776-1833 (MG 24, D4)
    Sir Frederick Haldimand Papers (MG 21, B2 — microfilm and transcripts from the British Library, London)
    Indian Records, vols. 1827-1834 (RG 10)
    Durell Saumarez Papers, 1777-1799 (MG 23, K10 — photocopies)
    War Office Papers (WO) 28 (MG 12, B — microfilm from Public Record Office, London)
Public Record Office, London, England
    Colonial Office Papers (CO) 5/253, "Secretary of State: Precis of Documents Relating to the Revolution, 1774-1777" (microfilm from the Library of Congress, Washington, D.C.)
    Colonial Office Papers (CO) 42, "Canada, Original Correspondence, 1700-1909" (microfilm copy at Public Archives of Canada, Ottawa)
    PRO 30/55, vols. 1010, "Headquarters Papers of the British Army in America (sometimes also called the Carleton Papers), 1775-1783" (microfilm at Lockwood Library, State University of New York at Buffalo)

War Office Papers (WO) 28, "Headquarters Records, America, 1746-1901" (microfilm copy at Public Archives of Canada, Ottawa)

War Office Papers (WO) 55/1537, "Letterbook, In and Out Letters, 1773-1777, Commanding Officer of the Royal Regiment of Artillery in North America (Lt. Col. Samuel Cleaveland, 4th Battalion, RRA)" (microfilm copy courtesy of Bernard R. Kazwick, Riverdale, Illinois)

The John Rylands University Library of Manchester, Manchester, England
    Caldwell Family Papers, Bagshawe Muniments

The State Historical Society of Wisconsin, Madison, Wisconsin
    Lyman C. Draper Mauscripts (microfilm copy)
        Series F. Joseph Brant Manuscripts
        Series S. Draper's Notes

William L. Clements Library, University of Michigan, Ann Arbor, Michigan
    Henry Clinton Papers
    Thomas Gage Papers
    Great Britain—Army in America
    Michigan Collection.

B. Published Documents, Correspondence, Journals, Memoirs, Travels, and Books

Askin, John. *The John Askin Papers, 1747-1820*, ed. Milo M. Quaife.
    2 vols.; Detroit: Detroit Library Commission, 1928-1931.

Badeaux, Jean-Baptist. "Invasion du Canada par les Américains en 1775." In *Invasion du Canada, collection de mémoires recuiellis et annotés par M. l'abbé Verreau, prêtre.* ed. Hospice Anthelme J. B. Verreau. Montréal: Société historique de Montréal, 1873.

Barnhart, John, ed. *Henry Hamilton and George Rogers Clark in the American Revolution, With the Unpublished Journal of Lieut. Govr. Henry Hamilton.* Crawfordsville, Ind.: R. E. Banta, 1951.

Baxter, James Phinney, ed. *The British Invasion from the North: The Campaigns of Generals Carleton and Burgoyne from Canada, 1776-1777, with the Journal of Lieut. William Digby of the 53d. or Shropshire Regiment of Foot.* Albany: Joel Munsell's Sons, 1887.

Boyd, Julian P., and Robert J. Taylor, eds. *The Susquehannah Company Papers.* 11 vols.; Ithaca, N.Y.: Cornell University Press, for the Wyoming Historical and Geological Society, Wilkes-Barre, Pennsylvania, 1930-1971.

British Army Lists, 1774-1784.

Burke, Edmond. *The Correspondence of Edmund Burke.* ed. Thomas W. Copeland *et al.* 9 vols.; Cambridge: At the University Press; Chicago: University of Chicago Press, 1958-1970.

Burton, Clarence M., ed. "Detroit During the Revolution." *Mississippi Valley Historical Review,* II (June, 1915), 118-120.

[Butler, John]. "Declaration of Colonel John Butler Received by Notary Beek, Montreal, 27 October 1787." *Rapport de L'Archiviste de la Province de Quebec pour 1924-1925* (Quebec: Ls-A. Proulx, 1925), pp. 393-396.

Caldwell, Henry, "The Invasion of Canada in 1775: Letter Attributed to Major Henry Caldwell." Literary and Historical Society of Quebec, *Manuscripts Relating to the Early History of Canada,* 2nd ser., V (1887), 1-20.

Caldwell, John. "Canada, 1776 and 1777: Two Letters from Detroit." *The Kingsman: The Journal of the King's Regiment,* n.s. VIII (Autumn 1975), 154-156.

Campbell, Patrick. *Travels in the Interior Inhabited Parts of North America.* ed. H. H. Langton. Edinburgh, 1793; republished Toronto: The Champlain Society, 1937.

Cohen, Sheldon S., ed. *Canada Preserved: The Journal of Captain Thomas Ainslie.* New York: New York University Press, 1969.

Cruikshank, Ernest A., ed. "The Journal of Capt Walter Butler on a Voyage along the North Shore of Lake Ontario from the 8th to the 16th of March 1779." *Transactions of the Royal Canadian Institute* (Toronto), IV, pt. 1 (1892-1893), 279-283.

Cruikshank, Ernest A., ed. *Records of Niagara, 1784-9.* Niagara Historical Society, Publication no. 40. Niagara-on-the-Lake, Ont.: Niagara Historical Society, [1929].

Davies, Kenneth G., ed. *Documents of the American Revolution, 1770-1783.* 2 vols.; Shannon and Dublin: Irish University Press, 1972-1981.

Day, Richard E., comp. *Calendar of Sir William Johnson Manuscripts in the New York State Library.* Albany: University of the State of New York, 1909.

De Peyster, Arent Schuyler. *Miscellanies, by an Officer.* Dumfries, Scotland: C. Munro, at the Dumfries and Galloway Courier Office, 1813; republished, ed. with app. and notes by J. Watts de Peyster; New York: C. H. Ludwig, 1888.

DeWitt, Charles G. "The Captivity of Capt Jeremiah Snyder & Elias Snyder, of Saugerties, Ulster Co., N.Y." *The Saugerties* [New York] *Telegraph*, V, nos. 13 and 14 (January 25, and February 1, 1851). The Garland Library of Narratives of North American Indian Captivities, vol. LXIV. facsim. New York and London: Garland Publishing, Inc., 1977.

Elmer, Ebenezer. "Journal Kept during an Expedition to Canada in 1776, by Ebenezer Elmer, Lieutenant in the Third Regiment of New Jersey Troops in the Continental Service, Commanded by Colonel Elias Dayton." *Proceedings of the New Jersey Historical Society*, 1st ser., II (1846-1847), 95-146, 150-194, III (1848-1849), 21-56, 90-102.

Enys, John. *The American Journals of John Enys*. ed. Elizabeth Cometti. Syracuse: Adirondack Museum and Syracuse University Press, 1976.

Fliegel, Carl John, comp. *Index to the Records of the Moravian Mission among the Indians of North America*. New Haven, Conn.: Research Publications, Inc., 1970.

Force, Peter, comp. *American Archives*: ... *a Documentary History of ... the North American Colonies*. 4th ser. (March 7, 1774-1776), 3 vols.; Washington, D.C.: M. St. Clair Clarke and Peter Force, 1837-1853. [no more published]

Gage, Thomas. *The Correspondence of General Thomas Gage with the Secretaries of State, and with the War Office and the Treasury, 1763-1775*. comp. and ed. Clarence E. Carter. 2 vols.; New Haven: Yale University Press, 1931-1933.

Grant, Francis. "Journal from New York to Canada, 1767." *New York History*, XIII (April-July, 1932), 181-196, 303-322.

Great Britain, Historical Manuscripts Commission. *The Manuscripts of the Earl of Dartmouth*. 3 vols.; London: Her Majesty's Stationery Office, 1887-1896.

Hadden, James Murray. *Hadden's Journal and Orderly Books: A Journal Kept in Canada and Upon Burgoyne's Campaign in 1776 and 1777, by Lietuenant James Murray Hadden; Also Orders Kept by Him and Issued by Sir Guy Carleton, Lieut. General Burgoyne, and Major General William Phillips in 1776, 1777, and 1778*. ed. Horatio Rogers. Albany: Joel Munsell's Sons, 1884.

Hadfield, Joseph. *An Englishman in America, 1785: Being the Diary of Joseph Hadfield*. ed. Douglas S. Robertson. Toronto: The Hunter-Rose Co., Ltd., 1933.

Hunter, Robert, Jr. *Quebec to Carolina in 1785-1786: Being the Travel Diary and Observations of Robert Hunter, Jr., a Young Merchant of London*. ed. Louis B. Wright and Marion Tinling. San Marino, Calif.: The Huntington Library, 1943.

Johnson, William. *The Papers of Sir William Johnson*. ed. James Sullivan, Alexander C. Flick, and Milton W. Hamilton. 14 vols.; Albany: The University of the State of New York, 1921-1965.

Kent, Donald H., and Merle H. Deardorff, eds. "John Adlum on the Allegheny: Memoir of the Year 1794." *Pennsylvania Magazine of History and Biography*, LXXIV (1960), 265-324, 435-480.

"The King's Shipyard." *Burton Historical Collection Leaflet*, II, no. 3 (January, 1924), 17-32.

Kirkland, Samuel. *The Journals of Samuel Kirkland: 18th-century Missionary to the Iroquois, Government Agent, Father of Hamilton College*. ed. Walter Pilkington. Clinton, N.Y.: Hamilton College, 1980.

Lajeunesse, Ernest J., ed. *The Windsor Border Region: Canada's Southernmost Frontier: A Collection of Documents*. Toronto: The Champlain Society, 1960.

La Rochefoucault Liancourt, [Francois Alexander Frederic], duc. de. *Travels through the United States of North America, the Country of the Iroquois, and Upper Canada, in the Years 1795, 1796, and 1797; with an Authentic Account of Lower Canada*. trans. Henry Neuman. 2 vols.; London: T. Davison, 1799.

[Lees, John]. *Journal of J. L., of Quebec, Merchant*. ed. M. Agnes Burton. Detroit: Society of Colonial Wars of the State of Michigan, 1911.

Lender, Mark E., and James Kirby Martin, eds. *Citizen-Soldier: The Revolutionary War Journal of Joseph Bloomfield*. Newark: New Jersey Historical Society, 1982.

Long, John. *Voyages and Travels in the Years 1768-1788*. ed. Milo M. Quaife. 1791; republished Chicago: R. R. Connelley & Sons Company, 1922.

Lorimier, Chevalier [Claude-Nicholas-Guillaume] de. "Mes services pendant la guerre américaine de 1775." In *Invasion du Canada, collection de mémoires recueillis et annotés par M. l'abbé Verreau, prêtre*. ed. Hospice Anthelme J. B. Verreau. Montréal: Société historique de Montréal, 1873.

Michigan State Pioneer and Historical Society. *Collections of the Michigan State Pioneer and Historical Society*. 40 vol.; Lansing: State Printer, 1877-1929.

New-York Historical Society. *Collections of the New-York Historical Society*. New York: New-York Historical Society, 1868-.

New York (State), Legislature. *Journals of the Provincial Congress, Provincial Convention, Committee of Safety and Council of Safety of the State of New-York, 1775-1776-1777*. 2 vols.; Albany: Thurlow Weed, Printer to the State, 1842.

Norton, John. *The Journal of Major John Norton, 1816*. ed. Carl F. Klinck and James J. Talman. Toronto: The Champlain Society, 1970.

O'Callaghan, Edmund Bailey, ed. *The Documentary History of the State of New-York*. 4 vols.; Albany: Weed, Parsons & Co., 1849-1851.

O'Callaghan, Edmund Bailey, and Berthold Fernow, eds. *Documents Relative to the Colonial History of the State of New-York*. 15 vols.; Albany: Weed, Parsons and Company, 1856-1887.

Parke, Capt. Andrew, J[acob] Maurer, and Hugh MacKay. "Account of the Events at the Cedars, Montreal, September 6, 1776 (certified correct by Capt. George Forster, Montreal, September 17, 1776." In *An Authentic Narrative of Facts Relating to the Exchange of Prisoners taken at the Cedars* ... London, 1777.

Pennsylvania Archives: Selected and Arranged from Original Documents in the Office of the Secretary of the Commonwealth ... ed. Samuel Hazard *et al.* 138 vols. in 9 ser.; Philadelphia and Harrisburg, 1852-1935.

Penrose, Maryly B., comp. *Indian Affairs Papers: American Revolution*. Franklin Park, N.J.: Liberty Bell Associates, 1981.

[Porteous, John]. "From Niagara to Mackinac in 1767." ed. F. Clever Bald. *Algonquin Club* [of Detroit] *Historical Bulletin*, no. 2 (March, 1938), pp. 1-14.

Redington, Joseph, and Richard Arthur Roberts, eds. *Calendar of Home Office Papers of the Reign of George III, 1760-1775, Preserved in the Public Record Office*. 4 vols.; London: Her Majesty's Stationery Office, 1878-1899.

Roche, John F., ed. "Quebec Under Siege, 1775-1776: The 'Memorandums' of Jacob Danford." *Canadian Historical Review*, L (March, 1969), 68-85.

Scribner, Robert L., Brent Tarter, and William James Van Schreevan, eds. *Revolutionary Virginia: The Road to Independence*. 7 vols.; [Charlottesville]: The University Press of Virginia for the Virginia Bicentennial Commission, 1973-1982.

Seaver, James E. *A Narrative of the Life of Mary Jemison: De-he-wa-mis, the White Woman of the Genesee*. First published 1824; 7th ed., with geographical and explanatory notes; New York and London: G. P. Putnam's Sons, The Knickerbocker Press, 1910.

Short, W. T. P., ed. "Journal of the Principal Occurences during the Siege of Quebec by the American Revolutionists under Generals Montgomery and Arnold in 1775-76 [Attributed to Sir John Hamilton]," London: Simpkin and Co., 1824. Reprinted pp. 55-101, vol. II, *Blockade of Quebec in 1775-1776 by the American Revolutionists (Les Bastonnais)*. ed. Fred C. Wurtele. Literary and Historical Society of Quebec, Seventh and Eighth Series of Historical Documents. 2 vols.; Quebec: Literary and Historical Society of Quebec, 1905-1906.

Shortt, Adam, and Arthur G. Doughty, eds. *Documents Relating to the Constitutional History of Canada*. 2 vols.; Ottawa: S. E. Dawson, 1907.

Sullivan, James, ed. *Minutes of the Albany Committee of Correspondence, 1775-1778*. 2 vols.; Albany: The University of the State of New York, 1923 and 1925.

Thwaites, Reuben Gold, and Louise Phelps Kellogg, eds. *Documentary History of Dunmore's War, 1774*. Madison: The State Historical Society of Wisconsin, 1904.

Tryon County, New York, Committee of Safety. *The Minute Book of the Committee of Safety of Tryon County* ... [August, 1774-November, 1775]. introd. by J. Howard Hanson and notes by Samuel Ludlow Frey. New York: Dodd, Mead and Company, 1903.

Verreau, Hospice Anthelme J. B., ed. *Invasion du Canada, collection de mémoires recueillis et annotés par M. l'abbé Verreau, prêtre*. Montréal: Société historique de Montréal, 1873.

"Virginia Legislative Papers." *Virginia Magazine of History and Biography*, WVI (July, 1908).

Wallace, William Stewart, ed. *Documents Relating to the North West Company*. Toronto: The Champlain Society, 1934.

Weld, Isaac, Jr. *Travels Through the States of North America, and the Provinces of Upper and Lower Canada, during the Years 1795, 1796, and 1979*. London: John Stockdale, 1799.

Wisconsin, The State Historical Society of. *Wisconsin Historical Collections*. 31 vols.; Madison: The State Historical Society of Wisconsin, 1854-1931.

C. Newspapers and Periodicals

Almon, John, ed. *The Remembrancer; or, Impartial Respository of Public Events*. 17 vols.; London, 1775-1784.

The Quebec Gazette (La Gazette de Quebec), 1774-1783.

II. Secondary Sources

A. Books

Alden, John R. *General Gage in America: Being Principally a History of His Role in the American Revolution.* Baton Rouge: Louisiana State University Press, 1948.

Alden, John R. *John Stuart and the Southern Colonial Frontier: A Study of Indian Relations, War, Trade, and Land Problems in the Southern Wilderness, 1754-1775.* Ann Arbor: The University of Michigan Press, 1944.

Allen, Robert S. *The British Indian Department and the Frontier in North America, 1755-1830.* Canadian Historic Sites: Occasional Papers in Archaeology and History, no. 14. Ottawa: National Historic Parks and Sites Branch, Parks Canada, Indian and Northern Affairs, 1975.

Armour, David A., and Keith R. Widder. *At the Crossroads: Michilimackinac during the American Revolution.* Mackinac Island, Mich.: Mackinac Island State Park Commission, 1978.

Bargar, B. D. *Lord Dartmouth and the American Revolution.* Columbia: University of South Carolina Press, 1965.

Beauchamp, William M. *A History of the New York Iroquois, Now Commonly Called the Six Nations.* New York State Museum, Bulletin 78. Albany: New York State Museum, 1905.

Bradley, Arthur Granville. *Lord Dorchester* [Guy Carleton]. The Makers of Canada Series, vol. III. Toronto: Morang & Co., Limited, 1907; plus later editions of 1926 and 1966 revised with critical appendices by Alfred L. Burt.

Brown, Gerald Saxon. *The American Society: The Colonial Policy of Lord George Germain, 1775-1778.* Ann Arbor: University of Michigan Press, 1963.

Burke, (Sir) John Bernard. *A Genealogical and Heraldic Dictionary of the Peerage and Baronetage of the British Empire.* 17th ed.; London: Hurst and Blackett, 1855.

Burt, Alfred L. *The Old Province of Quebec.* Toronto: The Ryerson Press; Minneapolis: The University of Minnesota Press, 1933.

[Cannon, Richard]. *Historical Record of the King's, Liverpool Regiment of Foot, containing an Account of the Formation of the Regiment in 1685, and of Its Subsequent Services to 1881; Also, Succession Lists of the Officers who Served in Each of the Regimental Ranks, with Biographical Notices and Summaries of Their War Services.* rev. ed.; London: Harrison and Sons, 1883.

Cannon, Richard. *Historical Record of the Seventh Regiment, or The Royal Fusiliers: containing An Account of the Formation of the Regiment in 1685, and of Its Subsequent Services to 1846.* London: Parker, Furnival, & Parker, 1847.

Chalmers, Harvey. *Joseph Brant: Mohawk.* East Lansing: Michigan State University Press, 1955.

Clarke T. Wood. *The Bloody Mohawk.* New York: The Macmillan Company, 1941.

Coffin, Victor. *The Province of Quebec and the Early American Revolution: A Study in English-American Colonial History.* Madison: University of Wisconsin, 1896.

Coupland, Reginald. *The Quebec Act: A Study in Statesmanship.* Oxford: Clarendon Press, 1925.

Cruikshank, Ernest A. *The Story of Butler's Rangers and the Settlement of Niagara.* Wellend, Ont.: Lundy's Lane Historical Society, 1893.

Curtis, Edward E. *The Organization of the British Army in the American Revolution.* New Haven and London: Yale University Press, 1926.

Dictionary of Canadian Biography (Laurentian Edition). Toronto, Buffalo, and London: University of Toronto Press, 1967-.

Downes, Randolph C. *Council Fires on the Upper Ohio: A Narrative of Indian Affairs in the Upper Ohio Valley until 1795.* Pittsburgh: University of Pittsburgh Press, 1940.

Dunnigan, Brian Leigh. *Seige - 1759: The Campaign Against Niagara.* Youngstown, N.Y.: Old Fort Niagara Association, Inc., 1986.

Flexner, James Thomas. *Lord of the Mohawks: A Biography of Sir William Johnson.* rev. ed.; Boston and Toronto: Little, Brown and Company, 1979.

Ford, Worthington Chauncey, comp. *British Officers Serving in America, 1754-1774.* Boston: Historical Printing Club, 1894.

Ford, Worthington Chauncey, comp. *British Officers Serving in the American Revolution, 1774-1783.* Brooklyn: Historical Printing Club, 1897.

Frey, Sylvia R. *The British Soldier in America: A Social History of Military Life in the Revolutionary Period.* Austin: University of Texas Press, 1981.

Fryer, Mary Beacock. *King's Men: The Soldier Founders of Ontario.* Toronto and Charlottetown: Dundurn Press Limited, 1980.

Graymont, Barbara. *The Iroquois in the American Revolution.* Syracuse: Syracuse University Press, 1972.

Halsey, Francis Whiting. *The Old New York Frontier.* New York: Charles Scribner's Sons, 1901.

Hargrove, Richard J. *General John Burgoyne.* Newark: University of Delaware Press, 1983.

Harvey, Oscar Jewell. *A History of Wilkes-Barré, Luzerne County, Pennsylvania, from Its First Beginnings to the Present Time; Including Chapters of Newly-Discovered Early Wyoming Valley History, Together With Many Biographical Sketches and Much Genealogical Material.* 3 vol.; Wilkes-Barré: Raeder Press, 1909.

Hatch, Robert McConnell. *Thrust for Canada: The American Attempt on Quebec in 1775-1776.* Boston: Houghton Mifflin Company, 1979.

Hodge, Frederick Webb, ed. *Handbook of American Indians North of Mexico.* Bureau of American Ethnology, Bulletin 30. 2 vols.; Washington, D.C.: Smithsonian Institution, 1907-1910.

Houlding, J.A. *Fit for Service: The Training of the British Army, 1715-1795.* Oxford: Clarendon Press, 1981.

Howard, Robert West. *Thundergate: The Forts of Niagara.* Englewood Cliffs, N.J.: Prentice-Hall, Inc., 1968.

Howson, Gerald. *Burgoyne of Saratoga: A Biography.* New York: Times Books, 1979.

Kellogg, Louise Phelps. *The British Régime in Wisconsin and the Northwest.* Madison: The State Historical Society of Wisconsin, 1935.

Kelsay, Isabel Thompson. *Joseph Brant, 1743-1807: Man of Two Worlds.* Syracuse: Syracuse University Press, 1983.

Ketchum, William. *An Authentic and Comprehensive History of Buffalo ...* 2 vols.; Buffalo: Rockwell, Baker & Hill, Printers, 1864-1865.

Lanctot, Gustave. *Canada and the American Revolution, 1774-1783.* trans. Margaret M. Cameron. Cambridge: Harvard University Press, 1967.

Lefferts, Charles M. *A History of the Uniforms of the American, British, French and Germans in the War of the American Revolution, 1775-1783.* New York: New-York Historical Society, 1926.

Luzader, John F., Louis Torres, and Orville W. Carroll. *Fort Stanwix: History, Historic Furnishing, and Historic Structure Reports.* Washington, D.C.: Office of Park Historic Preservation, National Park Service, U.S. Department of the Interior, 1976.

Lydekker, John W. *The Faithful Mohawks.* New York: Macmillan Company, 1938.

McIlwraith, Jean N. *Sir Frederick Haldimand.* The Makers of Canada Series, vol. VI. Toronto: Morang & Co., Limited, 1906.

McLean, John P. *An Historical Account of the Settlements of Scotch Highlanders in America prior to the Peace of 1783, Together With Notice of Highland Regiments and Biographical Sketches.* Cleveland: The Helman-Taylor Company; Glasgow: John Mackay, 1900.

Mathews, Hazel C. *The Mark of of Honour.* Toronto: University of Toronto Press, 1965.

Morgan, Lewis Henry. *League of the Ho-de'-no-sau-nee, Iroquois.* 1851; republished Secaucus, N.J.: The Citadel Press, 1972.

Neatby, Hilda M. *Quebec: The Revolutionary Age, 1760-1791.* Toronto: McClelland and Stewart Limited, 1966.

Norton, Thomas E. *The Fur Trade in Colonial New York, 1686-1776.* Madison: The University of Wisconsin Press, 1974.

O'Donnell, James H., III. *Southern Indians in the American Revolution.* Knoxville: University of Tennessee Press, 1973.

Parker, Arthur C. *The History of the Seneca Indians.* Rochester, N.Y.: Lewis Henry Morgan Chapter of the New York State Archeological Association, 1926.

Pound, Arthur, in collaboration with Richard E. Day. *Johnson of the Mohawks.* New York: The Macmillan Company, 1930.

Reynolds, Paul R. *Guy Carleton: A Biography.* New York: William Morrow and Company, Inc., 1980.

Roberts, Robert B. *New York's Forts in the Revolution.* Rutherford, Madison, and Teaneck, N.J.: Fairleigh Dickinson University Press, 1980.

Russell, Nelson Vance. *The British Régime in Michigan and the Old Northwest, 1760-1796.* Northfield, Minn.: Carleton College, 1939.

Severance, Frank H. *Old Trails on the Niagara Frontier.* 2nd ed.; Cleveland: The Burrows Brothers Co., 1903.

Shaw, Helen Louise. *British Administration of the Southern Indians, 1756-1783.* Lancaster, Pa.: Lancaster Press, Inc., 1931.

Smith, Justin H. *Our Struggle for the Fourteenth Colony: Canada and the American Revolution.* 2 vols.; New York and London: G. P. Putnam's Sons, 1907.

Sosin, Jack M. *The Revolutionary Frontier, 1763-1783.* New York: Holt, Rinehart and Winston, 1967.

Sosin, Jack M. *Whitehall and the Wilderness: The Middle West in British Colonial Policy, 1760-1775.* Lincoln: University of Nebraska Press, 1961.

Stanley, George F. G. *Canada Invaded, 1775-1776.* Canadian War Museum, Historical Publications, no. 8. Toronto and Sarasota: Samuel Stevens, Hakkert & Company, 1977.

Stevens, Wayne E. *The Northwest Fur Trade, 1763-1800.* Urbana: The University of Illinois, 1928.

Stone, William L. *Life of Joseph Brant - Thayendanegea: including The Border Wars of the American Revolution, and Sketches of the Indian Campaigns of Generals Harmar, St. Clair, and Wayne, and other matters connected with the Indian Relations of the United States and Great Britain, from the Peace of 1783 to the Indian Peace of 1795.* 2 vols.; New York: Alelxander V. Blake, 1838.

Sturtevant, William C., ed. *Handbook of North American Indians.* 20 vols.; Washington, D.C.: Smithsonian Institution, 1978-. Vol. XV, *Northeast,* ed. Bruce G. Trigger, 1978.

Swiggett, Howard. *War Out of Niagara: Walter Butler and the Tory Rangers.* New York: Columbia University Press, 1933.

Van Every, Dale. *A Company of Heroes: The American Frontier, 1775-1783. New York: Mentor Books, 1963.*

Van Every, Dale. *Forth to the Wilderness: The First American Frontier, 1754-1774.* New York: Mentor Books, 1961.

Wallace, Anthony F.C., with Sheila C. Steen. *The Death and Rebirth of the Seneca: The History and Culture of the Great Iroquois Nations, Their Destruction and Demoralization, and Their Cultural Revival at the Hands of the Indian Visionary, Handsome Lake.* New York: Alfred A. Knopf, 1970.

Waller, George M. *The American Revolution in the West.* Chicago: Nelson-Hall, 1976.

Wilson, Bruce G. *As She Began: An Illustrated Introduction to Loyalist Ontario.* Toronto and Charlottestown: Dundurn Press, 1981.

Wood, Louis Aubrey. *The War Chief of the Six Nations: A Chronical of Joseph Brant.* Chronicles of Canada Series, vol. XV. Toronto: Glasgow, Brook & Company, 1920.

B. Articles and Pamphlets

Abler, Thomas S. "Kaien'kwaaton [Sayenqueraghta]." *Dictionary of Canadian Biography* (Toronto, Buffalo, and London: University of Toronto Press, 1967-), IV, 404-406.

Abler, Thomas S. "Kayahsota' [Kayashuta]." *Dictionary of Canadian Biography* (Toronto, Buffalo, and London: University of Toronto Press, 1967-), IV, 408-410.

Abler, Thomas S., and Elisabeth Tooker. "Seneca." Pp. 505-517 in *Northeast,* ed. Bruce G. Trigger. Vol. XV of *Handbook of North American Indians,* ed. William C. Sturtevant. 20 vols.; Washington, D.C.: Smithsonian Insitution, 1978-.

Arthur, Elizabeth. "Henry Hamilton." *Dictionary of Canadian Biography* (Toronto, Buffalo, and London: University of Toronto Press, 1967-), IV, 321-325.

Boston, David. "The Three Caldwells." *The Kingsman: The Journal of the King's Regiment,* n.s. II (December, 1963), 316-317.

Bowler, R. Arthur. "Sir Guy Carleton and the Campaign of 1776 in Canada." *Canadian Historical Review,* LV (June, 1974), 131-140.

Bowler, R. Arthur, and Bruce G. Wilson. "John Butler." *Dictionary of Canadian Biography* (Toronto, Buffalo, and London: University of Toronto Press, 1967-), IV, 117-120.

Brand, Irene B. "Dunmore's War." *West Virginia History,* XL (Fall, 1978), 28-46.

Browne, Douglas G. "The Butlers of Butlersbury." *Cornhill Magazine,* n.s. II (November, 1921), 601-616.

Bryce, P. H. "Sir John Johnson, Baronet: Superintendent-General of Indian Affairs, 1743-1830." *The Quarterly Journal of the New York State Historical Association,* IX (July, 1928), 233-271.

Caya, Marcel. "Henry Caldwell." *Dictionary of Canadian Biography* (Toronto, Buffalo, and London: University of Toronto Press, 1967-), IV, 120-121.

Clifton, James A. "Merchant, Soldier, Broker, Chief: A Corrected Obituary of Captain Billy Caldwell." *Journal of the Illinois State Historical Society,* LXXI (August, 1978), 185-210.

"Colonel Arent de Peister." *The Kingsman: The Journal of the King's Regiment,* III (June, 1932), 4-5.

Conover, George S. *Sayenqueraghta: King of the Senecas.* Waterloo, N.Y.: Observer Steam Job Printing House, 1885.

Cruikshank, Ernest A. "Early Traders and Trade-Routes in Ontario and the West, 1760-1783." *Transactions of The Royal Canadian Institutie (Toronto),* III, pt. 2 (September, 1893), 253-274, IV, pt. 2 (December, 1895), 299-313.

Cruikshank, Ernest A. "Memoir of Captain Walter Butler." *Transactions of The Royal Canadian Institute (Toronto),* IV, pt. 2 (December, 1895), 284-298.

Curry, Richard Orr. "Lord Dunmore and the West: A Re-evaluation." *West Virginia History,* XIX (July, 1958), 231-343.

Downes, Randolph C. "Dunmore's War: An Interpretation." *Mississippi Valley Historical Review,* XXI (December, 1934), 311-330.

Dunn, Walter S., Jr. "The Frontier on the Eve of the Revolution." *Niagara Frontier,* XX (Winter, 1973), 96-111.

Dunnigan, Brian Leigh. *History and Development of Old Fort Niagara.* Youngstown, N.Y.: Old Fort Niagara Association, Inc., 1985.

Dunnigan, Brian Leigh. *A History and Guide to Old Fort Niagara.* Youngstown, N.Y.: Old Fort Niagara Association, Inc., 1985.

"La Famille Caldwell." *Le bulletin des recherches historiques,* XLII (January, 1936), 3-6.

Fleming, R. Harvey. "Phyn, Ellice and Company of Schenectady." *University of Toronto: Contributions to Canadian Economics,* IV (1932), 7-41.

Gibbs, Harley L. "Colonel Guy Johnson, Superintendent General of Indian Affairs, 1774-1782." *Papers of the Michigan Academy of Science, Arts and Letters,* XXVII (1942), 595-613.

Graham, Jane E. "Jean-Baptiste De Couagne." *Dictionary of Canadian Biography* (Toronto, Buffalo, and London: University of Toronto Press, 1967-), IV, 173-174.

Graymont, Barbara. "Thayendanegea." *Dictionary of Canadian Biography* (Toronto, Buffalo, and London: University of Toronto Press, 1967-), V, 803-812.

Hagan, William T. *Longhouse Diplomacy and Frontier Warefare: The Iroquois Confederacy in the American Revolution.* Albany: New York State American Revolution Bicentenenial Commission, 1976.

Hamilton, Milton W. "Joseph Brant—The Most Painted Indian." *New York History,* XXXIX (April, 1958), 119-132.

Hoberg, Walter. "Early History of Colonel Alexander McKee." *Pennsylvania Magazine of History and Biography,* LVIII (January, 1934), 26-36.

Hoberg, Walter. "A Tory in the Northwest [Alexander McKee]." *Pennsylvania Magazine of History and Biography,* LIX (January, 1935), 32-41.

Hultzén, Claud H. *Old Fort Niagara: The Story of an Ancient Gateway to the West.* Buffalo, N.Y.: Old Fort Niagara Association, 1933.

Kelsay, Isabel Thompson. "Joseph Brant [1742-1807]: The Legend and the Man, A Foreward." *New York History,* XL (October, 1959), 368-379.

Kerby, Robert L. "The Other War in 1774: Dunmore's War." *West Virginia History,* XXXVI (October, 1974), 1-16.

Macdonald, George F. "Commodore Grant." Ontario Historical Society, *Papers and Records,* XXII (1925), 167-181.

MacDonald, Kenneth R., Jr. "The Battle of Point Pleasant: First Battle of the American Revolution." *West Virginia History,* XXXVI (October, 1974), 40-49.

Macpherson, K R. "List of Vessels Employed on British Naval Service on the Great Lakes, 1755-1875." *Ontario History,* LV (September, 1963), 172-179.

O'Donnell, James H., III. "Joseph Brant." Pp. 21-40 in *American Indian Leaders: Studies in Diversity.* ed. R. David Edmunds. Lincoln and London: University of Nebraska Press, 1980.

Potter, William L. "Redcoats on the Frontier: The King's Regiment in the Revolutionary War." Pp. 41-60 in *Selected Papers from the 1983 and 1984 George Rogers Clark Trans-Appalachian Frontier History Conferences.* ed. Robert J. Holden. Vincennes, Ind.: Eastern National Park & Monument Association, 1985.

Quaife, Milo M. "Commodore Alexander Grant." *Burton Historical Collection Leaflet,* VI, no. 5 (1928).

Reibel, Daniel B. "The British Navy on the Upper Great Lakes, 1760-1789." *Niagara Frontier,* XX (Autumn, 1973), 66-75.

Reynolds, Neil B. "The Butlers of Wyoming and Cherry Valley." *The American Genealogist,* XXXVI (October, 1960), 201-203.

Rogers, E. S. "Southeastern Ojibwa." Pp. 760-771 in *Northwest.* ed. Bruce G. Trigger. Vol. XV of *Handbook of North American Indians.* ed. William C. Sturtevant. 20 vols.; Washington, D.C.: Smithsonian Institution, 1978-.

Rossie, Jonathan G. "Daniel Claus: A Personal History of Militant Loyalism in New York." Pp. 147-183 in *The Human Dimensions of Nation Making: Essays on Colonial and Revolutionary America.* ed. James Kirby Martin. Madison: The State Historical Society of Wisconsin, 1976.

Rossie, Jonathan G. "Guy Johnson." *Dictionary of Canadian Biography* (Toronto, Buffalo, and London: University of Toronto Press, 1967-), IV, 393-394.

Rossie, Jonathan G. "The Northern Indian Department and the American Revolution." *Niagara Frontier,* XX (Autumn, 1973), 52-65.

Sears, Stephen W. "The Lion's Eye View: A British Officer Portrays Colonial America." *American Heritage,* XXIX (June-July, 1978), 98-107.

Severance, Frank H. "With Bolton at Fort Niagara." Pp. 53-84 in Frank H. Severance. *Old Trails on the Niagara Frontier.* 2nd ed.; Cleveland: The Burrows Brothers Company, 1903.

Siebert, Wilbur H. "The Loyalists and Six Nation Indians in the Niagara Peninsula." *Transactions of the Royal Society of Canada,* 3rd ser., IX (1915), 79-128.

Smith, Donald B. "The Dispossession of the Mississauga Indians: A Missing Chapter in the Early History of Upper Canada." *Ontario History,* LXXII (June, 1981), 67-87.

Smith, Donald B. "Who are the Mississauga?" *Ontario History,* LXVII (December, 1975), 211-222.

Smith, Paul L. "Sir Guy Carleton: Soldier-Statesman." Pp. 103-141 in *George Washington's Opponents: British Generals and Admirals in the American Revolution.* ed. George Athan Billias. New York: William Morrow and Company, Inc., 1969.

Sosin, Jack M. "The British Indian Department and Dunmore's War." *Virginia Magazine of History and Biography,* LXXIV (January, 1966), 34-50.

Sosin, Jack M. "The Use of Indians in the War of the American Revolution: A Re-Assessment of Responsibility." *Canadian Historical Review,* XLVI (June, 1965), 101-121.

Stanley, George F. G. "Allan Maclean of Torloisk." *Dictionary of Canadian Biography* (Toronto, Buffalo, and London: University of Toronto Press, 1967-), 503-504.

Stevens, Paul L. "The Indian Diplomacy of Capt. Richard B. Lernoult, British Military Commandant of Detroit, 1774-1775." *The Michigan Historical Review,* XIII (Spring, 1987) 45-80.

Stevens, Paul L. "A Minnesota Dakota Chief in Quebec City, 1776: New Information Regarding Wabasha's Visit to the Governor of British Canada." *Minnesota History,* [to be published in a 1987 or 1988 issue].

Stevens, Paul L. "'Placing Proper Persons at Their Head': Henry Hamilton and the Establishment of the British Revolutionary-Era Indian Department at Detroit, 1777." *The Old Northwest, XII (Summer, 1986).*

Strach, Stephen G. *The British Occupation of the Niagara Frontier.* Niagara Falls, Ont.: The Lundy's Lane Historical Society, 1976.

Swiggett, Howard, "A Portrait of Colonel John Butler." *New York History,* XVIII (1937), 304-311.

Tooker, Elisabeth. "The League of the Iroquois: Its History, Politics, and Ritual." Pp. 418-441 in *Northeast.* ed. Bruce G. Trigger. Vol. XV of *Handbook of North American Indians.* ed. William C. Sturtevant. 20 vols.; Washington, D.C.: Smithsonian Institution, 1978-.

Vivian, James F., and Jean H. Vivian. "Congressional Indian Policy during the War for Independence: The Northern Department." *Maryland Historical Magazine,* LXIII (September, 1968), 241-274.

Walker, Mabel G. "Sir John Johnson, Loyalist." *Mississippi Valley Historical Review,* III (December, 1916), 318-346.

Wilson, Bruce G. "The Struggle for Wealth and Power at Fort Niagara, 1775-1783." *Ontario History,* LXVIII (September, 1976), 137-154.

Wise, S. F. "The American Revolution and Indian History." Pp. 182-200 in *Character and Circumstance: Essays in Honor of Donald Grant Creighton.* ed. John S. Moir. Toronto: Macmillan of Canada, 1970.

C. Unpublished Dissertations

Guzzardo, John C. "Sir William Johnson's Official Family: Patron and Clients in an Anglo-American Empire, 1742-1777." Ph.D. dissertation, Syracuse University, 1975.

Inouye, Frank T. "Sir William Johnson and the Administration of the Northern Indian Department." Ph.D. dissertation, University of Southern California, 1951.

Jaebker, Orville John. "Henry Hamilton: British Solider and Colonial Governor." Ph.D. dissertation, Indiana University, 1954.

LeRoy, Perry Eugene. "Sir Guy Carleton as a Military Leader during the American Invasion and Repulse in Canada, 1775-1776." Ph.D. dissertation, Ohio State University, 1960.

Pastore, Ralph Thomas. "The Board of Commissioners for Indian Affairs in the Northern Department and the Iroquois Indians, 1775-1778." Ph.D. dissertation, University of Notre Dame, 1972.

Stevens, Paul L. "His Majesty's 'Savage' Allies: British Policy and the Northern Indians during the Revolutionary War—The Carleton Years, 1774-1778." Ph.D. dissertation, State University of New York at Buffalo, 1984.

Venables, Robert William. "Tryon County, 1775-1783: A Frontier in Revolution." Ph.D. dissertation, Vanderbilt University, 1967.

ACKNOWLEDGEMENTS

A King's Colonel at Niagara derives, in one way or another, from the author's comprehensive, wide-ranging doctoral dissertation. Much of the text has been extracted and reassembled almost verbatim from that 2,500-page manuscript, and the remainder was based upon research materials gathered initially for that project. Consequently, *A King's Colonel* has been in the making since 1971, when random ideas about the Revolutionary frontier took the solid shape of a dissertation theme. During the succeeding years many individuals and institutions assisted the author's investigation of this topic.

Librarians and archivists in large numbers contributed their time and expertise to this work. The early stages of research were facilitated by the cooperation of the librarians at the Lockwood Library of the State University of New York at Buffalo and at the Buffalo and Erie County Public Library. Searches through various manuscipt collections were made with greater ease and profit because of the help provided by the staffs of the Public Archives of Canada, the William L. Clements Library, the Burton Historical Collection of the Detroit Public Library, and the Buffalo and Erie County Historical Society.

Much of the research was carried out through the mails and could not have been accomplished without the willingness of others to answer persistent questions and fill nagging requests for microfilms and photocopies. Particular acknowledgement is owed to several individuals in the United Kingdom, namely *Glenise A. Matheson* at The John Rylands University Library of Manchester, *E. J. Priestley* formerly at the King's Regiment Collection of the Merseyside County Museums in Liverpool, and *Desmond Donaldson* at the Ewart Public Library in Dumfries, Scotland. Also courteous and efficient in their assistance were staff members of the manuscript divisions of the Public Archives of Canada, the Archives of Ontario, the Pennsylvania Historical and Museum Commission, the Historicial Society of Pennsylvania, and the New York Public Library. In addition, useful research materials regarding the British military in the American west were graciously loaned by *Bernard R. Kazwick* and *William L. Potter,* active members of British units in the Northwest Territory Alliance (a Revolutionary War re-enactment association).

An academic fellowship at the D'Arcy McNickle Center for the History of the American Indian at The Newberry Library, Chicago, during 1979-1980 furnished the intellectual stimulation, library resources, and funds without which this would have been a much different and poorer study. The Center's staff, fellows, and visiting researchers and speakers succeeded in broadening the author's perceptions of all aspects of Indian and frontier history during a series of colloquia, seminars, and discussions, and a fieldtrip to Indian reservations in the northeastern United States. The personnel of the Main Reading Room and of Special Collections never failed to locate the rarest or most obscure publication. On many occasions *Helen Hornbeck Tanner* took time from her duties as editor of *The Atlas of Great Lakes Indian History* to share her impressive knowledge of Indian history. Special thanks must be extended to *Mary A. Druke,* Associate Director of the Center's documentary history of the Iroquois project, who patiently explained her own insights into the functioning of Iroquois society and politics in the eighteenth century.

Dedicated teachers at the State University of New York at Buffalo imparted an understanding of the interwoven strands of American, Canadian, and British history that proved necessary to comprehend Niagara during the American Revolution. Bolstering encouragement and beneficial suggestions were offered by Professors *Melvin J. Tucker, Milton Plesur, Robert G. Pope, Arthur Bowler,* and *Norman Baker.* For many years *Dr. Robert L. Ganyard* steadfastly supervised and guided the author's research and writing. To him is owed special gratitude for the latitude to pursue that research without undue restraints and for the careful, time-comsuming critiques that improved that writing's grammar, organization, and logic.

The staff and volunteers of the Old Fort Niagara Association provided unflagging support and indispensable assistance at every step of the process of transforming the typewritten manuscript into the finished publication. Through his thorough familiarity with all aspects of Fort Niagara and its dependencies, Executive Director *Brian Leigh Dunnigan* saved the author from a number of errors about the Niagara Frontier during the British regime. *Harry DeBan,* Chairman of the Publications Committee, contributed a huge amount of time to design and produce this work. Other committee members, *David Bertuca, Craig Burt, John Burtniak* and *Richard Cary,* proofread copy and otherwise aided in the production. *Mr. Paul Huey* of the New York State Bureau of Historic Sites read the original manuscript and offered his comments and suggestions. Typesetting was done by *Karen Conti.* Invaluable production support was provided by the *Niagara Gazette.*

Lastly, the sincerest appreciation must be expressed to the author's parents, *Stanley Francis Stevens* and *Mary Louise Oechslin Stevens,* without whose understanding, patience, and financial support he could not have completed this study.